L FOR THE LOVE OF GOD AND FAMILY

Finding Joy while Caregiving

Martha H. Robertson

ISBN 979-8-88751-767-4 (paperback)
ISBN 979-8-88751-768-1 (digital)

Christian Faith Publishing
832 Park Avenue
Meadville, PA 16335
www.christianfaithpublishing.com

Printed in the United States of America

In memory of Lou Ellen Hardman Henry (my mother),
Edward and Barbara Robertson (my
father in-law and mother in-law),
Aunt Maggielene Robertson (my partner in crime,
as staying out of trouble was hard to do)
to whom I owe my inspiration.
See you later, alligators.

ACKNOWLEDGMENTS

Jesus, you sent me on this journey, and I believe you set my heart on this book and wouldn't let me put it in a box with all my well-intentioned but never finished projects. I pray this book honors your will in the lives of both the caregivers who read it and the loved ones being cared for.

I would like to thank my very sweet friend and comrade in the role of caregiving as she cared for her mother and daddy. I am positive God brought us together. Thank you for the multiple times you read my manuscript. You even reread an old version because my computer had some kind of crazy glitch, taking the time to make changes that had long been rewritten. Then you went back and read the current one without even batting an eye. If that isn't friendship, I don't know what is. You helped me organize my notes and made suggestions when I found myself struggling to make my intended point. You helped me with my grammar and listened to my unending stories. Your encouragement gave me the confidence to share it with others. Donna Avery Andrews, my friend, I can never express what you have meant to me!

Lynnette Dunn, your encouragement started me back to working on this project after I had wavered on whether my experiences and observations were relevant to other caregivers' reality. Also, you made some very useful suggestions that helped clarify some ideas on how to organize my thoughts so "the cart didn't come before the horse." Thank you for suggesting I add the section on grief. To me, that is the most important emotion you have to confront before you can be consoled into the caregiving role. You were the best to take the time and consideration to read and contribute to this project. I truly, truly thank you! I actually only met you twice face-to-face, but I know God orchestrated those meetings, and I thank him for that! Thank you for the support you provide caregivers through Piedmont Sixty Plus Services. You are a gift from God!

To Tori Sorrells, I love how you always know the right thing to say when loved ones reach out to you when facing hard decisions or just needing a shoulder to cry on. Your sensible and loving advise makes it possible for these daughters, sons, brothers, sisters, husbands, wives, or friends to persevere with a little less guilt and a lot more confidence and strength. God put you here and God sent me to you. I know it!

Katy Economou, you have been a blessing in so many ways, from helping Aunt Maggielene get back on her feet from COVID-19 to teaching me how to go forward in making everyday activities continue with therapeutic results. Never doubt your God-given gift. Thank you for reading this manuscript and encouraging me to go forward with it. You are amazing!

Thank you to my *older*, wiser brother, Raleigh, and his wife Patty who double-checked the scripture to make sure the verses I used truly complimented the content. I know you spent hours reading this manuscript. I love you both!

Aunt Maggielene, I wouldn't take anything for the memories of the days we spent together. Not only that, your children have proven to be the ultimate example of family working together, keeping each other confident in their decision on the care of their mother. (Thankfully, you and Uncle Allen began the process with them before it became their total responsibility.) Brent, Scott, Kevin, and Tammy never doubt it was the right decision for you. By combining the roles of a memory care facility with the extra companionship of a caregiver, you were able to spend your time with your mother, sharing laughter and sweet moments while forging great memories that will last a lifetime. You spent your time creating joy for your mom and removing the feeling that she might be a burden while you made me, as the caregiver, feel appreciated and loved. In turn, I found myself falling in love with you. Aunt Maggielene, you have forever changed my life. Our days together were the sweetest! I will forever treasure them. Tammy, Kevin, Scott, and Brent, you have my heart.

Kathleen Goulos of Christian Faith Publishing, thank you for our lengthy conversations on the challenges of caring for loved ones and your assurance that this is a season of life that requires the support and validation of those who have gone before.

Emily Hope of Christian Faith Publishing, you kept me aware that I was in the middle of a project that wasn't going to make a bit of a difference if I didn't get to work and see it through. Thank you for your sweet reminders.

To the editors of Christian Faith Publishing, thank you for the work you put into this project to help me offer this as a reliable tool for new caregiving families.

Tony, Jesse, and Ethan, my family, without you, this book would not have been written. Your patience and encouragement have been beyond generous. I love you very much!

CONTENTS

Introduction

Family

I was born into a Christian family. Most people refer to me as being a little sheltered. It is true; although our family had no less drama than any other.

I have always been particularly sensitive to other people's feelings, losing sleep over friends and family I knew were hurting or had been wronged. I was subject to feel a little melancholy and found that finding something to do to serve someone else seemed to be the answer to relieve some of the blues I found filling my days. Sometimes, my efforts were recognized and appreciated, but sometimes, I found, people suspected an ulterior motive. This made me want to give up. I wanted to make things right for folks, but I was finding it hard.

One day, I was in church when the pastor asked if anyone had anything to share that they had learned about

God. "You know the attributes of God and can recite them, now how do they apply to real life?" This lady raised her hand and said, "I know that no matter what I say, or how bad I mess up, God can make something wonderful from it." Wow! Now everything I have regretted saying and all the good intentions that have failed and all the bad decisions I made, whether intentional or not, may not make me a complete failure in life. In fact, something wonderful may have happened because of them. (I knew I still had to practice tact and social graces—still working on them. I pray for God to help me honor him in all my actions, words, and thoughts. Sometimes, I fail horribly.)

I still struggle to remember that, but I am sleeping better and I do feel days are more constructive. The thing is that now, I can take those things I have true passion for and trust God to make something truly wonderful from whatever I do. I know now; God wants me to stick my neck out and try to help people find joy in their lives. So therefore, here is my attempt to encourage you, the hero of your care receiver, to find joy in this very hard role in life or find joy despite the very hard road you are having to travel now.

God is who it has taken for me to do it.

"Come to me, all who labor and are heavy laden, and I will give you rest. Take my yoke upon you, and learn from me, for I am gentle and lowly in heart, and you will find rest for your souls. For my yoke is easy, and my burden is light" (Matt. 11:28–30 ESV).

Where each caregiving situation is unique, it is often that when listening to other people's accounts you think, "Yep, I know exactly what you are talking about." The situations may be different, yet the struggles are often the same.

My name is Martha Robertson, and I am going to attempt to share my story. I am the daughter of Walter and Lou Ellen Henry and the daughter-in-law of Edward and Barbara Robertson. What a great privilege to be able to claim this legacy! Both my parents and my husband's parents made great impacts on their communities just by loving and caring for their families and neighbors.

God blessed their children and grandchildren by letting them see their hard work and persistence in both how they supported, provided for, and expressed their love by their sacrifices for each other, their children, and their grandchildren. You would never have heard any of them say a negative word about any member of their families unless it was through heartbreaking tears, maybe not literal tears, but you always knew their hearts were aching with sorrow. Their pride in their children and grandchildren would shine with gratitude toward God for finding it his pleasure to bless their offspring, sometimes through hard lessons used to refocus their lives. Even though it was only through faith that God knew the outcome that they could be consoled, waiting with hope was what they did.

"But they who wait for the Lord shall renew their strength; they shall mount up with wings like eagles; they shall run and not be weary; they shall walk and not faint" (Isa. 40:31 ESV).

It has been a blessing to have the opportunity to be a part of my mother's and my in-laws' lives as they reached the last chapter in their earthly existence. I am probably the last person my mother or my in-laws would have imagined being as much involved in their final years, but how could I stay away from the very ones who God handpicked to use to grow me, my husband, and my children into the characters we are today. I say *characters* because I can just hear our friends and extended families say, "That family is made up of some real characters."

Well, I say, "Thank you, God, for blessing us with such strong beginnings."

My mother passed away in 2009, and I, along with my brothers and sisters, had the honor of being by her side when she drew her last breath. What a gift it was to be present when God released her soul from her broken-down, worn-out, cold body to the warm, secure, loving, everlastingly peaceful embrace of heaven. The rug that had been pulled out from under her by time and disease was replaced by the secure love of God's gift of eternal life.

Don't get me wrong; she didn't have a look of serenity on her face, and she wasn't able to express any endearing last words or gestures. Instead, she had been on a ventilator for a week or two; her face was contorted and rigid with her head leaning back and her mouth frozen open from holding the breathing tube. It was not the way I would have wanted to see my mother pass away, but when the struggling breath and that deep cough she could never really carry all the way through because of the breathing tube stopped, I knew she was healed. Just like that, she was happy and in the presence of the Great Physician. What joy I felt for her! Thank you, Jesus!

"Yes, we are of good courage, and we would rather be away from the body and at home with the Lord" (2 Cor. 5:8 ESV).

I miss her, but my heart is full of joy knowing she has our God caring for her firsthand, not that he was not before, but she was embossed in a perpetually decaying human body. He didn't choose to heal her earthly body because there wasn't any need. She was ready to continue her life with her Lord in glory.

My mother was the strongest woman I have ever known. You know the song "Daddy's Hands" by Holly Dunn? Well, that was a song sang at my daddy's funeral, but you could easily have replaced "Daddy's" with "Mama's." You hear people say, "I don't know how she does it." Well, I was there, and I still don't know how she did it. She was a city girl, who, after high school, used her income to help provide for her family until she married my father and abruptly transitioned to farm life. In fact, her prize gift at her bridal shower was a pig she promptly named Solomon and turned into a pet. For many years, she worked to help support the farm, but when she wasn't at her job, she was at home caring for us and farming.

Years later, after moving off the farm, but still living in the country miles from town, my mother worked forty hours a week at the Georgia Diagnostic and Classification Center, worked a large garden from which she froze, canned or pickled, and preserved all the vegetables she could; nothing was wasted. She catered weddings while five children, along with numerous cousins, and friends were constantly underfoot. She also helped with homework, school projects, and many times, she was the one who made sure the animals were loved and cared for. Daily, she had three meals on the table prepared by her hands. There were no fast-food establishments, and even when there were, we lived miles out of the way.

My mother was a great seamstress, and until we were older, she made most of our clothes. Her day started long before ours and many times ended during the early morning hours. Wow! When my father died tragically in January of 1989, she pulled her bootstraps up and lived her senior years to the fullest and encouraged her widowed friends to do the same. She was amazing!

She was the most courageous woman! She went from never ever spending a single night by herself to living by herself after the death of my father. She was sixty years old, and her house was large, with the constant creaks and whines of an old house. Sometimes the pressure in the house might cause a door to open or the stairs to creak. But that didn't hinder her decision to learn to weather out those long lonesome nights by herself.

For most of that time, she made all of her own day-to-day decisions, rarely asking for advice. (Not me, if it weren't for my husband, I wouldn't know how to handle any minor catastrophe.) Although during her final years, she was aware that my brothers had contacts for practical home maintenance and legal contacts she found useful. Now, I know her fear was much greater than I ever imagined—not fear of imminent danger, but fear of the unknown. She persevered, knowing that if she were to give in, that would mean the end of her independence, and her independence was that important to her! Her having what she wanted was important to me. God was her solid rock.

"Therefore everyone who hears these words of Mine and acts on them, may be compared to a wise man who built his house on the rock. And the rain fell, and the floods came, and the winds blew and slammed against that house; and yet it did not fall, for it had been founded on the rock" (Matt. 7:24–25 ESV).

If I could have a do-over with Mama, I think I would start with this letter, or maybe, I would have had a heart-to-heart talk with her.

Although I don't know that I could have gotten through the whole thing without making us both cry, me for admitting that I needed her, and her for hearing how much I needed her and how much she would have to depend on us.

This is not how it went, and I will always regret my lack of sensitivity to what my mother was facing. She was a rock star!

Dear Mama,

I just want to let you know how much I love you. You have been my stalwart example of what it means to take life on and thrive. For this, you have my greatest respect. Time has taught me that you are part of what makes me unique. Not to mention, I owe you my life.

I know that you are so confused about the next step in life. And I know you are skeptical of every change you have been forced to make, but I also know that I want to be with you, taking each step by your side.

This is sooo hard, but together we can work it out arm in arm and heart to heart. We will be happy, and we will meet our future together with the knowledge that we are partners in this very adventurous next chapter in the story of *our* lives. With God's light and God's guiding hand, we will make it, growing in love and respect for each other.

I plan on our future being one of shared laughter and long walks with long talks. I plan to get to know you in ways I have never even thought of until now. Don't even think of trying to make me move on because I'm not going anywhere.

We will need help, lots and lots of help. But this will mean you and I can have quality time when I come to visit (which will be often).

I love you and always will, no matter what! We are going to ride this thing out like it is a gift that will see us grow closer than we have ever been. This is our time; let's live like there is no tomorrow! I love you, Mama.

Sincerely,
Martha

Now, about four years after my mother passed away, Mr. Robertson, my father-in-law, was hospitalized with a urinary tract infection and aspiration pneumonia. This has really intensified his already developing dementia. It is obvious that Mrs. Robertson needs help to manage her new caregiving role. My homeschooled, younger son just graduated from high school, and I have not yet found a new job; therefore, I find myself becoming part of their very adventurous new normal.

It is plain to see that my in-laws have reached a much-feared and lonesome time in their lives. Mr. Robertson is in an advanced stage of dementia and mostly only understands that those around him love and care for him. This he sometimes (more often than not) finds to be a nuisance and tries to help them get over their willingness to work to keep him comfortable, happy, and healthy. He has always been the one caring for everyone else, and after all, these are the same people he changed diapers and switched when they misbehaved. Now, they are trying to boss him! I don't think so!

As the onset of dementia began to upset his ability to remain independent, he became a very angry, belligerent man. He was on the front line during the Korean War (police action), and he suffers from PTSD, which no one even suspected until he began to show signs of dementia. He cries for the loss of his friends, wondering if he had done enough to save them.

His best friends are those he fought side by side with during the war and reunited with decades later. So on many days, his thoughts are, "Why should I listen to some know-it-all busybody when I have gone to war, chased and shot at people, been chased and shot at, and lived through atrocities you would never be able to understand?" He told me this one day. From his point of view, there isn't anything I could say that would even seem logical. It is all true, but I care. So I keep trying to help make it okay.

Yet on good days, he is very loving, enjoying a sweet hug and kiss every once in a while. He puts on his best manners for company. He loves company! I always say his mother's training shines through brilliantly for friends and extended family. At this point, that pretty much includes anyone who isn't on hand regularly. It is always interesting to see what each day is going to bring because there is no way to guess. It has truly been a treat to be a part of this stage in his life.

As my father-in-law's dementia progresses, he still needs to know it is his home, and he is still the man of the house. It is important to me that he remains the head of the house as long as we can make it happen without taking away from his well-being. So if someone is sitting in the chair he wants to sit in, that person gets out, and he sits there. If he wants to walk rather than ride in the wheelchair, and if I can assist him enough to keep him safe, he walks.

Mrs. Robertson, on the other hand, is a treat of her own. She worries, and her anxiety levels are much too intense for her to continue to lead a normal, healthy life. She sees the worst possible outcome of any situation. Because of this, she rarely sees the touch of God's blessings during any given day. She misses so much! She is paralyzed with the fear she is going to do something wrong.

She is the most giving woman I know. Whenever someone says, "Boy, I love that," she will say, "Why don't you take it? I don't know what I would ever do with it" or when you ask, "May I borrow this?" she will say, "Sure, why don't you keep it? I never use it anyway."

She is very afraid of offending anyone. I love staying with them and find it hard to ever say "no" to them. At the same time, she expects her family to regard her as their priority. She needs to know she is first in their lives. They are first in hers!

Her children grew up to be hard workers. There are four children, all of which are totally different, yet they have undeniable similarities. They were reared on farm-work. The whole family pitched in and made their home a working farm. Mrs. Robertson knew her role as a helpmate for Mr. Robertson, and Mr. Robertson knew his role as a provider and caretaker for his wife and children. The only motivation they had was their love for each other and their children.

It is through this experience that I have learned of the fear our parents feel when they realize they are no longer the ones everyone depends on to babysit, help with household chores, come to the rescue at work, with transportation, or just a listening ear. They are now the ones needing help. Their world has turned upside down in just a blink of an eye.

It is also hard for the children to recognize the parents' true abilities and their need for assurance. These are the very people to whom these same children counted on for wisdom, comfort, and security.

We need to reflect on who they were and learn to love who they have become because that is who God has blessed us with for now. A great way of doing this is to write down the "used to be" to understand the "here and now." I believe this is a necessary process to be able to get a grip on the true capabilities and disabilities of our most loved ones. If they never complained and always committed to doing the hard "right thing" in the past and now are refusing to participate in the simplest tasks, they probably can't physically or mentally carry out these tasks.

My in-laws are the perfect example of what is meant by the wife being the helpmate and the husband being the provider. From the beginning, my mother-in-law made sure the house was always in order, the clothes were washed, the children tended to, and the food was on the table—everything to his satisfaction and more. My father-in-law made sure she was provided for the best he knew how. Anything she asked for she got if he could manage it. He knew what she was to him, and he depended on her for his every breath. You could see it in his eyes. Even now when he is in the advanced stage of dementia, all she desires for herself is that he is comfortable and happy! I have rarely seen these traits to this extent in any couple. It is the most beautiful thing I have ever witnessed.

> By wisdom a house is built, and by understanding it is established. (Prov. 24:3 ESV)

> Husbands, love your wives, as Christ loved the church and gave himself up for her, that he might sanctify her. (Eph. 5:25 ESV)

I love it when they sit on the front porch and watch the squirrels and the birds on the feeders. (I know you are supposed to run the squirrels off, but the hours of entertainment are well worth the dollars of birdseed.) God bless those squirrels as they perform for the two lovers sitting hand in hand, sometimes cuddled up on the front porch, in a world all their own admiring the beauty and music of the songbirds, the majestic flight of the hummingbirds, and the acrobatics of the squirrels and chipmunks.

I told my mother-in-law she should give seminars on how to honor, respect, and love your spouse. During my father-in-law's progression of dementia (even the belligerent, hateful days), she sat and held his hand, kissed and comforted him. When everyone else found they were feeling defensive and intolerant of his actions, his wife, even when deeply hurt and offended by his actions, would kiss and comfort him with the most loving forgiveness and with a gentle and tender heart. They were together over sixty years, or these days, you need to specify *married*. They didn't need time to see if it was going to work. They committed themselves to each other and never looked back. I think the secret was they were always most concerned about doing what was right for the other one.

> She opens her mouth with wisdom,
>   and the teaching of kindness is on her
> tongue.
> She looks well to the ways of her household
>   and does not eat the bread of idleness.
> Her children rise up and call her blessed;
>   her husband also, and he praises her:
> "Many women have done excellently,
>   but you surpass them all."

Charm is deceitful, and beauty is vain,
 but a woman who fears the Lord is to be
praised.
Give her of the fruit of her hands,
 and let her works praise her in the gates. (Prov.
31:26–31 ESV)

Likewise, husbands, live with your wives
in an understanding way, showing honor
to the woman as the weaker vessel, since
they are heirs with you of the grace of life,
so that your prayers may not be hindered.
(1 Pet. 3:7 ESV)

I have concluded that God is finally ready for me to
grow up because it has changed everything in my mindset
of what life is all about and what my role in this life is.

Courage and Faith

The first thing you need to accept is that this *is not
about dying.* This *is about living,* living a life that accepts
changes, living a life that brings on challenges, living a life
that brings vulnerability to your heart, living a life that reaps
the riches of seeing your loved one find joy and encouragement through your tender touch and soft heart.

I know you may be saying, "This is not my case because
they just don't want my help, and they don't hesitate to let
me know that every day." That is probably true, but this
may not be about them (hopefully, it is). This may be about
you. Your efforts of trying to make their lives easier with a

loving heart and a giving attitude defines your sincerity and your devotion. This may be about you either facing each day with the dread of caring for this awful disease, or waking up each morning knowing this is a new opportunity to serve and try to give joy to someone living in what seems a world that is slowly becoming foreign and lonely. It could be that it takes a very creative, imaginative plan that doesn't include your hands-on care to find this contented environment for your loved ones.

Your caring for your loved ones doesn't always mean your constant presence. It could mean your figuring out a way for someone else to take care of the hard, mundane, everyday challenges while you use your time to protect and assure your loved one's joy and find a way to give her/his life purpose. It just requires your love, efforts, and sincere intentions.

"Be joyful in hope, patient in affliction, faithful in prayer" (Rom. 12:12 NIV).

During your lifetime, there will be many life-altering events, but none exposes your heart more than being put in the role of caring for a spouse, a parent, or other loved one. This is the time you discover who you are and what you are made of. This is when you find out if you have the courage and faith to take your loved one's hand and lead her/him into what seems like an abyss, knowing that while you have her/his hand, God has his love wrapped around your loved one. God is taking that journey with you as he grips your hand leading the way.

> Have I not commanded you? Be strong
> and courageous. Do not be frightened,

and do not be dismayed, for the LORD your God is with you wherever you go. (Josh. 1:9 ESV)

Behold, God is my salvation; I will trust and will not be afraid; for the Lord God is my strength and my song, and he has become my salvation. (Isa. 12:2 ESV)

Looking in from the Outside

Looking in from the outside is hard because you only see what they want you to see. Or when you visit or call, it is a treat, and they can rise to the occasion seemingly with little difficulty. Yet you notice something is just not right with the house. The dishes aren't their normal clean. The animals aren't groomed or fed as well as usual. Their clothes aren't well matched. She doesn't cook their meals anymore. They're mostly eating sandwiches. Their house is no longer spotless. And you start getting little snippets of things that don't seem exactly right. When you check into it, you realize it has been this way for a while, and it is continually getting worse.

Sometimes, it is hard to know when to step in. All I know is, there are signs if you are on hand enough to notice changes in your parents' routines. They don't seem content any longer. Yet when you visit, everything seems okay. There is no real reason for things to be like they are. They don't seem physically sick. They can hold their end of the conversation, but they just aren't themselves. It could be they are slowing down and just need some help around the house. This is when you need to start spending more time there helping them.

The only way you're going to know how your parents are is to spend enough time to see them respond to everyday routines. Spend the day, weekend, or better yet, a week with them. Participate in their everyday activities. Be there when they get up in the morning. Fix breakfast with them. Sit with them through the morning, enjoying the fact that you are spending your day with the most important people in your life. These are the very people who brought you into this world, loved you more than anyone else ever could, and fought for your well-being all the way up to the point where they need you to fight for them.

Eat lunch with them, wash dishes, and sit with them through the afternoon, sharing your life and learning of their lives and history. They love for you to show interest in where they came from and what they lived through. They love the chance to reminisce with someone truly interested. Treat them to a supper planned and prepared by you. And then, sit with them until bedtime saying good night with a firm hug and a purposeful kiss.

Don't make your visits the same all the time. Why not work to give them a very special week enjoying cooking together, shopping, and caring for the animals. Go to a movie; visit friends and family. Make memories for them and you. When you do this, keep in mind that your visit is a treat, and they are likely to be rising to the occasion. They are excited over the extra attention you are giving them, and they want to make this visit enjoyable for you. If you see areas of concern, know these are even of more concern when they are by themselves. Therefore, it may be time to think about getting them some help. If they are very independent people, they are not likely to ask for help. They may not be willing to accept their inability to manage on their own. It is important you provide help now because the sooner the help comes, the easier the transition and the sooner they will settle into a new normal.

(From this point on, I will be using the pronouns *she* and *he* or *his* and *her*. Note that these pronouns can easily be interchanged. Caregivers nor care receivers are gender-specific.)

Now What?

So now, it has been decided that Mom and Dad need help. They are no longer capable of dealing with the everyday ins and outs of their routine on their own. Or maybe, there is only one who is debilitated to this degree. At this point, it is important to establish to what extent help is required. Maybe, for now, they only need someone hanging around for a little distraction from the reality of their life changes, or it may be, they just need someone to provide transportation and/or grocery shopping.

What is really difficult is when one member of the couple is totally physically and mentally capable of doing all the things required to provide their care, yet she is emotionally paralyzed. Common sense says she just needs to get a grip and come to terms with the situation. She should learn to cope while finding joy in her responsibility.

Just know, there is no way she is going to come to terms with the fact that the person who provided security, the one who has kept their lives stable and their family together, the one who in the middle of a trial held her in his arms, assuring her everything was going to be okay, would not be there to help her care for him now. How can she accept she is going to have to do this on her own?

As time goes on and the necessity for help progresses, you will need to make visits at least a couple of times a month. Let them know when you will be coming so they can look forward to it. Do this even if you have several other siblings doing the same thing because your parents will react to each one of you differently. Each one will have his own insight into the needs and concerns of your parents. (Each concern when broached should be taken seriously because the smallest things can mean so much to the care receiver.) Your parents deserve this time with you. Use this time to put a caregiving plan together and to discern when it is time to reevaluate the plan.

Caregiving Plan

So now that everyone agrees they need help, how do you provide this help? Are you capable of supplying their needs? What are your other obligations? Are you going to emotionally be able to cope with their growing dependence on you? Do you have what you would consider time to care for them? (Where it is said that you always have time for those things important to you, there are several options for you to consider that could result in you giving your loved ones the best care while your available time is spent loving on and enjoying them.) Are you physically capable of providing care for them? Are you, or they, in a financial situation that will support your hands-on care? Are you willing, really willing?

If any of these questions wave red flags, flicker light bulbs, supply dread, or seem a little overwhelming, you probably need to search for help to teach you how to care for your loved ones or provide the service of caregiving (to what extent depends on the amount of burden you are willing to take on). The word *burden* should probably be replaced by *responsibility* (no matter what word you use, you need help) because you should in no way consider taking on this task without knowing it will bring an abundance of joy to care for those who gave you the best of themselves the majority of their lives.

To take this on, you have to be emotionally ready to handle the frustration, sadness, anger, grief, and uncertainty of change every day. On the other hand, you should not feel guilty for deciding they need more professional and trained caregiving than you can provide.

Every situation is different, and everyone has his own gifts, none greater than the other. You need to decide what is best for your parents. It could be you want to use your time with them to visit and enjoy loving on them by sharing recreational activities. In that case, someone, or many other people need to do the chores. It could be finding the right long-term care facility to manage the laborious stuff is the best way to go. It surely is the way to lift the day-to-day mundane worries from your shoulders. Have peace in this decision! You are caring for your parents by providing a way for them to feel less of a burden to you. But don't think you won't be regularly involved in making decisions and keeping a sharp eye to make sure medicines are getting distributed right and prescriptions are changed when necessary because you definitely will. You will probably need to make sure personal hygiene is managed as needed because things just fall through the cracks if your attention to these details falter. Eyes on your loved one regularly will be imperative for the best care to be provided in a facility.

How Do I Manage?

Don't immediately be overwhelmed with what is coming. I know it seems like you are going to be thrown into something so overwhelming when you first get the diagnosis of dementia, Parkinson's, cancer, or another debilitating disease; but you don't have to know how to cope with everything now. You will grow into your new role as time requires. What seems new and intimidating, more than you can do today, becomes second hand tomorrow. All you have to do each day is get through the day. Go at a pace that your care receiver sets. You can do it! Just make your decision and stick to it—no guilt, no second guesses. Your loved one will adjust, given time. And believe it or not, they will love you for standing up and taking the burden of everyday life from them once they do adjust to all of the radical changes having to be made. They may never tell you, but you will see them relax and wear their new role well (at least, if their disease affords them the chance to notice their change).

Decision Made

You decide you can do this. It is what is right for your mom and dad. You have taken on the responsibility of being your parents' caregiver. *Care* is the operative word here. You have to want to love on and care for your parents in ways you are used to being cared for by them. The only thing is that they are not your children; they are your parents. They will not be learning to eventually care for themselves. You will not be training them. Every day they will lose a little bit more of the skills they have taken for granted, and any adult is expected to do with ease. You still have to treat them with the same respect and authority they have always had, but you also have goals to accomplish. You have to figure out how to reach these goals while letting them feel the love and respect they have earned.

Caregiving is a full-time job; I don't care if there are a half dozen of you caring for your mom and dad. You need to be aware of their everyday habits, both their daily routine and their ability to cope with their routine. Taking turns is not enough because there will be times when their routines may have to be altered, and their care will require a change to accommodate their needs. Therefore, everyone should be on hand to observe how your parents react to each of you. Each one will have a very individual relationship with your parents.

It may be they listen and respond to one child's suggestion better than the others that they need to change a particular habit. It may be that they will only let one child take care of their hygiene. One of you may know how to cook just what they love. Another may be more playful and exciting to be around than the rest. Keep in mind that you can use these relationships to manipulate any given situation to accomplish its goal. On the other hand, one of you may cause more anxiety and need to take a break every now and then or change the way you approach a situation. It may be that that person's role in the caregiving process should be redefined.

Adjust to the Moment

If your parent is refusing to cooperate with his regular caregiver, sometimes, it is helpful for that person to back off and let another person give it a try. It doesn't matter who gets the job done as long as it gets done. This is important for times when you have to give him medicine, keep him fed and hydrated, change his clothes, or take him to the bathroom. It is not a reflection of who does the best job or who is liked the most. Many times, it has to do with the mood at the moment. Or perhaps, he is enjoying the person he is with at that time. Tomorrow, it may be quite the opposite.

When it comes to hiring a caregiver, be willing and able to do everything you ask the caregiver to do because you have no idea how hard it is to do the seemingly simplest task unless you have tried yourself. If he won't let you, then know he might not let the caregiver, or he might be willing to let her and not you or vice versa. Or it could be one minute he will, but the next minute, there is no way.

Your relationship with your loved one may contribute to whether he will or will not let you perform certain tasks; therefore, you may be forced to rely on someone else to achieve some goals needed to make your loved one comfortable and safe. All these are great reasons for you to realize the importance of your participation in every aspect of caregiving at least every couple of weeks—every couple of weeks because things change.

In the Loop

It is very important to keep everyone who's involved in the caregiving informed of arrangements being made for doctor's appointments, plumbing issues, transportation needed, and grocery shopping. This way, no one will be making appointments on top of someone else's, causing confusion and sometimes embarrassing situations. No one will be wasting time or automobile fuel running unnecessary errands or creating unnecessary work for the others involved. In other words, be considerate! Also be repentant when it is your fault that time and effort are wasted.

Remember, this is not a time to put value on each of the caregivers' time. Each person's time is just as valuable as the others. It doesn't matter how it is spent; it is his time. It doesn't matter if you have five school-age kids. The others' time is just as valuable as yours. If they wind up having to put in more time and energy than you, it is up to you to find a way to compensate. If they have spouses who step in and help, then maybe you have a spouse who can give some of his valuable time, or maybe you could find a way to give the more involved caregiver a special day by springing for an outing or dinner at a nice restaurant.

No Perfect Manual or Caregiver

Of course, there are no manuals on how to provide or manage the care for your particular parent because everyone reaches these final years by a unique path. Each brings into this season his own exceptional past. Personalities play a great role in the consideration of how to care for your parent. Is he strong-willed or meek and mild-mannered? Is he fun or fearful? Is he secure or needy? Also, your financial situation could limit your options greatly.

Even if you can pay for the best facility or the luxury of a full-time caregiver, don't let that give you the false confidence to leave your parent in the care of someone else without plenty of input from you. Stay ever knowingly present. In other words, make your potential presence be forefront. They need you! Of course, as the comfort of a dependable, secure, and trusting relationship emerges between you and your caregiver, you have the confidence to relax and lean on your newly (hopefully) honorary family member. By the way, you can pay bundles of money and still be provided rotten care. Your parents deserve the best! They deserve you!

I don't mean to not have a paid caregiver or enlist the help of a caregiving facility! Of course, caregivers are a great gift, and one that stands alone in its value for allowing a loved one peace of mind. I just mean you are what makes having a caregiver work. Do your homework, ask the right questions, know exactly what you need, and figure out a way to communicate that to your new caregiving ally. It doesn't have to be so hard, stressful, nor wearisome with the right fit for a caregiver. Everyone stays informed and massages the others' willingness to serve by sincerely caring for the other involved caregivers.

There may not be that perfect instruction manual written for particular strategies you should take to direct and lead your parents into a safe and happy environment especially designed for them. But the Bible is a manual on how you should honor, respect, obey, and love your parents. This is serious business, and God is giving you the opportunity to love your parents in a way that no one else can. And they need to know you love them. I promise you, you will be so grateful to have had the chance to openly show your parents what their being part of your life has truly meant to you.

> You shall stand up before the gray head and honor the face of an old man, and you shall fear your God: I am the Lord. (Lev. 19:32 ESV)

> Honor your father and your mother, as the LORD your God commanded you, that your days may be long, and that it may go well with you in the land that the LORD your God is giving you. (Deut. 5:16 ESV)

World Turned Upside Down

Is This Really Happening?

What has happened to this man who has spent most of his life caring for you? Is he expecting you to take over and mother him like you would your children when you were training them to care for themselves?! He knows better. And what is worse is when he is indignant about the whole thing.

If you can keep all this from getting under your skin and not blow your top, you are better than most anybody else and need to be fitted for sainthood. It is hard to realize you are not training him because this is all about his losing his trained skills. His mind is declining; there is nothing you can do about it, and nothing he can do about it. He really can't help it. Until he becomes less able to do these things that seem irrational and difficult to manage, it will get worse.

While each person's journey into the path of the disease is unique, it is vital that you take the time and effort to seek out knowledge and understanding by reading books and articles, talking to professionals and friends with experience, gleaning insights from those who have traveled this road before you. Joining a support group is one of the best ways to make these contacts.

During my time of caring for my in-laws, I became aware of a support group sponsored by Piedmont Sixty Plus, a program put together to aide in the care of seniors in the community. This support group focuses on families who care for loved ones with dementia. Here, I have listened to the family members' funny stories, heartbreak, laughter, hurt feelings, endearing anecdotes, tears, embarrassment, exhaustion, hearts overflowing with love, confusion, and the joy of accomplishments well done. But mostly, I hear of love, compassion, and efforts to find answers to challenges which seem to be as diversified as the hours in the day. I have grown to truly care for these folks who have dug their heels in the trenches determined to pour their love out on their care receiver whether at home or in a facility.

I don't know if Sixty Plus actually officiates a support group anymore because of changes brought on by COVID-19, but I do know that they can direct you to one of many good groups out there.

Joining and participating in one of these groups will give you an idea of what is to come and insight on how to prepare for the mental and physical progressions. It will help take away some of the fear when the sun sets, the house settles down for the night, and your thoughts wander into the realm of panic, as you try to see into a future which is both unpredictable and undetermined. Only God has this insight, so know this: "Therefore do not be anxious about tomorrow, for tomorrow will be anxious for itself. Sufficient for the day is its own trouble" (Matt. 6:34 ESV).

I want to assure you that you don't have to worry about what tomorrow will bring until tomorrow because what you are dealing with today is hard enough. What seems hard today you will find yourself doing by rote tomorrow, and today will most likely prove to be harder than what you will be faced with as the disease progresses. For one thing, today, you are adjusting to the new normal of facing each day as its own day with no regularity or predictability (no warning, no rhyme, no reason).

I'd like to share one heartbreaking account of a widow who came to meet, fall in love, and marry an exciting, adventurous, adoring, and doting widower. Only a few years in, he was diagnosed with dementia. They had only begun to make a life together when she quickly became a caregiver for a man she had known for a relatively short time, spending more years as a caregiver than a wife. What a heroic woman she was taking on her new role as a devoted partner with the love she committed to on her wedding day! She treasured those moments when he looked at her with the love they shared from the beginning. When he smiled, her heart melted. Still, it was too hard to care for him without the help and encouragement from others. She needed someone else to handle much of the hard stuff, which she seldom had, but she hung in there through sickness and death, not regretting a moment of the years spent doing the hardest, most tiring job in the universe, caring for her beloved. You know what? She had already done this for her previous husband.

Adjusting Spousal and Parental Roles

Whether your relationship began sixty years ago or last year, his position in your relationship hasn't changed at all in his mind, but you have morphed into the caregiver. Just be careful how you choose to approach this situation because you need his confidence and trust. Without them, your job is going to be much harder. He is truly not in his second childhood because if he were you could spank, scold, or use your authority over him to get him to reach your goals. But in his mind, you are still under his authority, or at any rate, he is your equal; and he is still your spouse, parent, or at least, you have an ongoing, caring, adult relationship. Otherwise, you wouldn't be here. So you learn manipulating, cajoling, and patronizing ways to meet goals. If you are very fortunate, you may just need to reason. All these things take patience. No, your roles are not reversed; they are just more complicated, intense, tiresome, and frustrating. But you must always remember your status in the relationship. None of the rules used to rear a child are going to get you the results you are looking for now—at least not in the long run. You may even leave a subconscious impression, if not a direct memory, of the humiliating way in which he was dealt, causing bad behavior in the future.

Nevertheless, you try to reason out how you are going to cope. At first, you may feel strong and capable, saying, "I've got this! My loved one has been diagnosed with dementia, and I'm the one he wants to care for him. Everyone else is busy with work, school, church, charities, children, and families of their own. He is mine! He has always been mine! I'm the one he wants! I'm the one he trusts! No one knows better than I how to care for him. Or there is no one else."

The Toll of the Caregiving Role

It is so easy to say that staying with your loved one is not hard. I have the time, and I am here. I can put off those things I need to do today until tomorrow or next week, and everyone else is busy. Well, guess what! Tomorrow and next week are going to bring on new issues and new challenges. You work until you become so exhausted you don't realize how tired you really are, and that is when you become detrimental to the loved one because you are not as alert as you should be to provide all his needs, and you are dangerous to function in what should be normal routine activities like driving home from the doctor's office, organizing medicine, or making decisions about the care receiver's mobility.

Even though you don't realize you are exhausted because you are focused on what you have to accomplish, you are no longer capable of reacting to traffic situations. You put yourself and others in danger. Or you forget his pain medicine, and it takes four hours to get him comfortable again. You might be so tired you reason that since your care receiver has been doing so well walking today, you will let him head to the bathroom by himself, and he falls. Sure, you are doing well for the rest of the care receiver's family, and they are letting or encouraging you to keep it up, but you are wearing yourself down and, in the end, not doing the best for your family after all.

Stop

So before you get in this kind of state...stop! Think about what you are saying; of course, staying with your loved one is going to be hard, especially if you are there all the time, and you can't continually put things off because next week never comes! Other challenges are just around the corner. Yes, you want to care for him. True, no one knows his likes and dislikes better than you. Of course, he trusts you more than anyone else! But you need rest and a clear, rational mind, which is not possible without relief and a little (a lot) of fun in your own life. Ask for help! If no one is able or willing to take some of the load, there is only one thing to do. Let go of those things that are not crucial to making your care receiver and you content and well cared for! Either hire someone to help or make a list of priorities, and don't worry about those things that are not essential. The only thing you have to do is make sure you and your loved ones are safe and cared for. Give yourself a break!

You have your personal needs, your caregiving responsibility, your own family obligations, and your work accountability. *All of these things matter* and need thought and structure for efficient handling.

You can't neglect your other obligations to be consumed by this very important, worthy, and endearing responsibility; although it is very easy to be swept up into loving the way out of the rest of your life. You have to balance your time and your strength to carry on with your other life. It is not going to be easy because at first, there will be guilt from passing on some of the duties you felt you were the only one who could do satisfactorily. Next, the guilt will come from not including him in all of the activities he once considered dear. But know you are doing the right thing for you, and these things no longer have the same meaning to him.

Know When to Ask for Help

I know it is hard to step back and watch someone else do the things you are used to doing and those things you know he wouldn't like anyone else to do, but you can't keep it up. So don't start out by saying, "I can do this." It is true you can do it now, but it becomes easier and easier to volunteer because you love him. And even when things weren't exactly perfect between you, now he is dependent on you, and you love doing for him. It can consume your every breath until you start to suffocate. That is why it is important to form a plan where you can engage others to help, maybe other family members, and divide the responsibilities out equally if at all possible. You will be guarding your emotional health along with your physical well-being. If you don't, you will find yourself making irrational decisions that can cause even more difficulties and frustration. Or you could be facing serious health issues of your own (stroke, heart attack, high blood pressure, diabetes, just to name a few).

It is definitely harder (too hard) for you to do what the two of you were doing with ease. For you to understand all you are taking on, here are a few important jobs you are probably not considering when you initially decide you can provide for your parent, spouse, or other loved one at home. And believe it or not, each of these things is important for making your care receiver comfortable in his home because many of these chores were chores he made sure were done when he was able. If they are not done properly, it will worry him to death; he might decide to get out and do the jobs himself. The other jobs are to keep you and your family on an even, balanced, and contented emotional plane.

Of course, that does not mean for you to take away all the activities he is still capable of doing. If he is not advanced enough in his disease to be unable to do these chores, don't stop him from maintaining his comfortable routine. The longer he remains coherent and physically able to carry on, the easier it is for you to physically manage him, and the more content he will be.

Breaking Down What You Need Help With

1. Grocery shopping
2. Cooking (meal preparation)
3. Developing menus
4. Doctor's appointments
5. Transportation
6. Medicine (pick-up and distribution)
7. Bathing
8. Therapy when necessary during the week
9. Therapy on weekends
10. Scheduling (meals, baths, doctor appointments, grocery shopping, transportation, business appointments, therapy, etc.)

11. Companionship for care receiver
12. Activities for care receiver
13. Holiday caregiving
14. Special occasion responsibilities
15. Trash pickup
16. Legal matters
17. Bank issues
18. Insurance
19. Keeping in touch with friends and family
20. Being flexible with caregiving when the scheduled caregiver is absent because of sickness or personal reasons
21. Home maintenance
22. Car maintenance
23. House cleaning (especially bathrooms)
24. Landscape maintenance
25. Loving your family
26. Staying content with your role
27. Having compassion and loving the one you are caring for

Therefore, before you get established as his primary caregiver, you need to face the reality of needing help, lots and lots of it. Bring in other family members or friends. Tell them you need their help! Have them talk to professionals with you. Don't assume they are taking your word for it. If they are not living in it, they have no idea, and they are going to be hard to convince. They need at least two days in your place, without your intervention if possible. You need to go somewhere for a couple of days. Go to the beach. Kick back for a weekend; you don't know when you will get back, so relax knowing someone who cares for your spouse/parent/loved one is there caring for him and getting a good education on what you do every day.

It doesn't matter whether you are the paid on-hand caregiver or not, if you are the spouse or another live-in family member, I stress again strongly, you have to have help! You need time to take in what is happening and to somehow be able to find joy in this new phase of life. You can't do that if you continue to keep life glued together by yourself. Do not misunderstand me; you are the primary caregiver, but that means you set the tone. You know what is needed. Therefore, you make sure there is someone there who will meet all of the caregiving needs, plus knows you are the boss.

You need to be able to feel free to receive the smile your loved one tries to share with you and respond to the tears when he needs to know he is not as big of a burden as he feels he is. He needs every hug you can muster and the companionship he has had with you for so many years. You can't give him that, nor do you feel like giving him that if you have been cleaning up spills or food thrown across the room when he has found something on his plate he doesn't like, or when he doesn't make it to the bathroom on time and you have to clean him, the floor, the furniture, and yourself. You don't have the energy, nor do you have the inclination. Remember, you don't have all the know how to hold your current world together. Your job is to be there for his and your emotional well-being. That is number 1 on your list of things to do.

Primary and Relief Caregivers

If you decide to be the paid full-time caregiver, you need to set boundaries because if you are caring for your loved ones, you don't have the time nor the energy to take care of all the ends and outs of keeping life—in general—

running smoothly. It is totally possible if you explain the jobs needed to be done, your relief caregivers won't mind pitching in at all. If you are the one there most of the time and you don't clue the other caregivers in on what it is going to take for them to give the help you need, it is likely you will wind up doing much more than you should have to. If the other caregivers leave a job long enough, you will do it. Or all the dirty jobs no one else wants to do will be yours. That is exactly what you are trying to avoid. However, remember you are getting paid, and you should keep busy and be considerate to the other caregivers volunteering their time.

If you are one of the relief caregivers, do your share! Notice I said, "Do *your* share." No one wants to feel taken advantage of. Every caregiver's personal goal should be to care for the care receiver and the other caregivers. When you are there, do your best to make the next person's transition easier. If you do this with a giving attitude and an appreciation for your fellow caregivers, you will find much gratitude coming your way, and much satisfaction with your new, temporary normal—"temporary" being the operative word. So do your share, and if needed, more. Because your main goal is caring for your loved one. Sometimes caring for your fellow caregivers is a great way to show you care about your new role and your loved one.

Helping More than the Care Receiver

When working with others who are also freely giving of their time, patience, and love to the care receiver, remember to keep in mind that any small or large task you find to do would free up the next person to accomplish another needed chore or to spend extra time with your loved one. Everyone feels appreciated in his role if each caregiver says to himself, "If I do this, then she won't have to," rather than "If I don't do it, someone else will," or "It's not my job." If they are your parents, all of it is your job. Be thankful you do not have to do it all. Everyone has a life outside of the life of the one being cared for, and yours is not the most important.

"Do nothing from selfish ambition or conceit, but in humility count others more significant than yourselves. Let each of you look not only to his own interests, but also to the interests of others. Have this mind among yourselves, which is yours in Christ Jesus" (Phil. 2:3–5 ESV).

Know Each Caregivers Strengths

Once the decision is made to keep your loved one at home, a family member should be chosen to take the lead on organizing the care and maintenance for the person and the house. Besides the obvious caregiving time, there are chores no one wants to do, and you need to dole this work out to those who took on the responsibility of helping. Make a schedule of what needs to be done and how often. Assign your team certain jobs according to their ability and gifts. As a rule, time should be the determining factor for each member's contribution. Remember everyone's time is equally valuable, including your own. Your time is precious. Guard it carefully.

Although the care receiver may resist help, over time, he will adjust. The sooner this is done, the easier it is to adjust and the sooner you are settled into a comfortable routine.

Let's say there are six children helping with their parents. Yet someone on your team is not able or willing to physically help with the obligations. He should consider financially providing his share through an outside source. If necessary for him to be able to afford the extra help, you could keep a record of how much is spent to provide his share of the work and make a distribution from his part of the inheritance. You want to make sure everyone does his best to do his share and avoid strained relationships. For instance, hire someone to do routine lawn maintenance. Hire a housekeeper one day a week. Believe me, it is worth the extra money (if necessary) and may even save money when the stress and anxiety of keeping up causes your own health and safety issues.

Of course, there are reasons for someone not to be able to contribute; say for instance, someone lives out of commuting distance, doesn't make the income to provide the salary for hired help, and there is no inheritance. Then he should not be expected to contribute in those ways, but he could spend time on the telephone visiting with his loved one, making calls to set up doctor appointments, paying the bills, getting the loved one's affairs in order, and keeping up with extended family. And if no one is there during mealtime or when medicine is taken, he could call at the appropriate times to make sure this is done. You can't put the same obligation on that person, but he should be considerate of those who are taking on the majority of the load by going out of the way to help where he can.

(Again, as you read this book, know that the pronouns *he/she*, for caregiver and care receiver are exchangeable. It is written with specific pronouns only to make the reading smoother.)

Be Honest

Let's say everyone decides to pitch in and help with the caregiving. Are *you* really totally all the way 100 percent ready to give 70 percent of the time required to provide your parents or other loved ones with what they need? Because that is about what your share will probably be. Everyone has good intentions, but let's face it: life happens. Work, social engagements, children, grandchildren, church, all numbers of things that have always been very important parts of your life have to be put on a back burner for a season.

To some people, this is the natural course, an acceptable fact, as reality sets into the consuming responsibility of caregiving. They realize by taking this very rewarding and very demanding turn in the road of life, they have to replace much of their personal time with time caring for *their parents* or other care receivers. Others are not as willing and don't see the point when someone else is willing. It doesn't matter if that someone else's whole world is turned upside down to do what is needed as long as their own schedule is not compromised. I know this seems hard, but just ask the person who is available and willing to help after a year about his admiration, commendation, and regard for his fellow caregivers. It becomes hard to do for your loved ones, even though you see the need and you love caring for them, when you know the others are standing on the sidelines watching and saying, "As long as he wants to do it, let him go for it."

All you want to do is say, "I'm tired. You do it for a change and let me enjoy the sweet visits." That is reality. So if your attitude has turned sour, it's time for someone else to step in. It may be that it is time to consider another alternative.

Most caregivers who put their loved ones on top of their priority list find it to be the hardest yet most rewarding experience ever. The sideliners are never going to have the satisfaction of knowing when their parents really needed them, they did their part with no regrets.

> Do all things without grumbling or disputing, that you may be blameless and innocent, children of God without blemish in the midst of a crooked and twisted generation, among whom you shine as lights in the world, holding fast to the word of life, so that in the day of Christ I may be proud that I did not run in vain or labor in vain. (Phil. 2:14–16 ESV)

Professional Help

When my father-in-law was in his last stages of Parkinson's-related dementia, his hospice nurse told me it was time for his nurse son to step back and be the son and let her be the nurse. The family's part in caregiving is to be persistent in finding competent qualified doctors, nurses, and healthcare providers whom they can trust to make responsible decisions concerning that loved one. There needs to be someone who can say the treatment does or does not benefit the quality of life over the effort and anxiety of providing the treatment. Give yourself a break and let another professional help you make decisions. You concentrate on loving on your parent or other loved one and feeling the emotions this point in life requires. It's okay because you're not the one who ultimately has control over what is going on; God is. There is nothing you can do that God can't do without you. So relax and let yourself feel. The only way you are going to find peace is to find yourself totally dependent on God. When something does happen, you can't beat yourself up over it. God has your back, and if you are doing your best to help your loved one live a safe, functional, quality life, you are doing great!

4

Who Are They?: Take the Time to Find Out

His Eyes
Martha Robertson

His face has aged and his mind is broken,
But his eyes sometimes sparkle with love
    now unspoken.
His eyes flash an instant of that love as a
    token,
Of the years they have lived and the mem-
    ories spun,
The dreams they have shared as their lives
    were but one.
Her steadfast love will never end,
But, oh, to be back in the days of when…

It is important for us kids to remember our parents are still not only valuable but invaluable. Our parents are, you know. Even in advanced frailty, they are the ones who are really interested in our everyday lives. They are the ones who want to hear details and anecdotes from our families' lives. When they ask how we are doing, they aren't looking for "Fine. How are you?" They want half an hour, detailed update on what we have been doing. It is important for them to be able to share this time with us. Now is the time. *Take the time*, before dementia robs you of the opportunity!

It doesn't matter if you have ten siblings; you are special to your parents in your own way. They miss you when you are not there. They want you to visit. They want to be important to you. You are important to them. If you drop in for a few minutes and leave with tons to do, you give them the impression that you are only satisfying your conscience and not truly interested in them. You can make time for them just like you can make time for hobbies or other entertainment. Maybe for a season, you should make your loved ones the thing that you save your time for. Take the challenge of making their evening with you the best they could possibly have. Look ahead, plan, and find joy in making them feel as if they are worth your time because *they are*! Don't make them have to make excuses for you like "She has more important things to do than spend time with us" or "They are too busy to check on us." You always have time for your priorities, and they should be a very special priority. You are theirs. Put your heart into your time with them.

Our parents are the ones who mean it when they say they are praying for us. Not only that, they pray unceasingly and with fervor every day. No one else, no matter how close they are to us, is going to do that. How special our parents believe we are no matter how badly we mess up! We can't find that anywhere else.

When our children grow up and decide they need space and need to be independent, self-sufficient adults, it is our parents who empathize and find us coming back to them for reassurance that we have done our best. They have been there and have struggled with the same doubts and insecurities we have now. Now, we need to be there for them with reassurance that we are there emotionally ready with support, understanding, and compassion during this unsure time in their lives. We need to remind them over and over that we love them and *want* to care for them.

When our parents, who have always been independent and seemingly indestructible in their everyday lives, show signs of fear because of aging issues (dementia, Alzheimer's, body frailties, or anxiety), know this is real. Our parents seem to be drowning in a fish tank, thinking all of us other fish are looking on unconcerned, living our days without any thought of the struggle they are living out. It may be we, the other fish, nibble and pick on the drowning fish, trying to get them to liven up; our parents try, but they just don't have it in them any longer. The only ones they have to turn to have no way of understanding.

Their children and grandchildren have always seen them as the rocks who have created the very existence they use as their foundation. How could these same mentors be so pitiful? They seem to turn into dependent children, and we act like frustrated parents at our wits end. Our parents seem to be afraid to do anything, make decisions of their own, or carry out the simplest task without confirmation and approval. Or it could be they use manipulation to get their way. It could be they are frustrated because they don't feel they are being heard. It seems silly to us. Yet the fear that brings them to this place in life is real.

Who are they? They are the ones who need to feel like they matter to us. These independent people have lost their way so gradually that sometimes we miss what is right in front of us. They have been and always will be the ones God blessed us with, and we should still recognize them as a blessing from God.

We spend time doing the very best things for others, yet we don't see the need in our own world. It's true, we get caught up in doing community service, and we are so dedicated to showing our face at church or publicly organized good deeds where we get pats on our backs, and everyone knows he can depend on us. That is a great feeling, but… how is it we enjoy doing these things and not see the needs closest to us? Why do we put the needs of our own to the side and find the time for friends or acquaintances who would or could have any number of other people assist them? Or why do we watch others help those who are our responsibility with the attitude of "if they are doing it, all the better for me." It doesn't matter that another person is putting aside his obligations, or just as valuable plans to serve on our behalf. These are *our* people who need *us* to love them into tomorrow wherever that may lead.

As our parents age, there are many decisions that will have to be made. No decision is wrong if we spend time and communicate well with everyone participating in the caregiving. Just remember, we want what is best for all, whether it is a long-term facility or staying at home with a caregiver.

Grief

We have looked at who the care receiver is. Now, we must understand who we are as caregivers. We must embrace our roles with determination to be able to move forward with loving compassion toward our loved ones.

You try for weeks, months, even years to snap your loved one out of it. Then one day, what everyone has been telling you finally socks you right in the gut. The person you loved, depended on, idolized, cared for, and who cared for you is nowhere to be found. The body is there, the face is there, the life is still flowing through this person; but this is not your loved one.

Then you realize when you refer to common activities you shared as "the last time" (the last time we cooked dinner, went driving, set on the swing and watched the sunset, went on vacation, went to church, had a good conversation, enjoyed our grandkids, hosted the family Christmas together, or even enjoyed a good gibe) was really the last time, forever. Your heart breaks! "How could this have happened without my realizing? If I had only known to pay attention, I could have remembered every detail of the 'last time.' Why can't I remember? Why didn't I make it special?"

Tears, gut-wrenching tears.

It doesn't matter how well you have it together or how much you prepare, until you walk the trail, you have no concept of the boulders you have to climb, the stumps you will trip over, or the quicksand you will have to swim out of.

When Mrs. Robertson talked about caring for her husband who lived with dementia, she said, through tears, "I have known people with dementia, and I have been told of peoples' experience with dementia, but I had no idea of what it was or felt like to care for someone with dementia until I experienced it myself."

You don't have to imagine what it would be like to sit beside, bathe, feed, and care for someone who only resembles your loved one in face and body. All the attributes that really made him or her your special person has been buried in a bunch of personality and actions that resemble your loved one very little, if any. You will forever only be able to experience life together as caregiver—care receiver. You've had to say goodbye to the person you've depended on and developed a relationship with for what seems like forever. Then you have had to replace him or her with someone totally dependent on you to hold life together without disrupting the comfort and security of that person. Where do *you* find comfort and security?

Then the thought of what you have lost and what you have to do to go forward scares the daylights out of you. "How can I do it? I love this person, but this is not the person I love." Or "I know the person I love is sitting beside me loving me but struggling to find the words to let me know because to him the words no longer exist."

Tears, gut-wrenching tears.

You try to talk to someone about it. They either act like you are overdramatizing or you should be able to suck it up. It's just part of life. Right?

God hasn't put this time on you to give you the opportunity to prove your devotion for this most important person. God hasn't put this on you to punish either of you. God has not given you this time as an opportunity to prove your love and trust in God's good will (even though you have that, it still hurts). God hasn't provided you long, weary days and sleepless nights worrying, dreading, and praying for this to go away because he has no compassion.

What he is doing is using it to grow you. What God has done is given you the need to cry out to him for help. He has opened the door for you to petition him to grow you in wisdom, confidence, patience, peace, love, humbleness, and total dependence on him.

Jesus has endured it all. In fact, he endured all of every sin ever committed by me, you, your loved one, and everyone else in the universe from all times—past, present, and future all at one time, in one single act of sacrifice. He literally became our blood sacrifice. He knows what suffering is. Jesus is the only one who can carry us through the foggy tunnel of dementia as he takes our hands in his and walks before us shining his light on our paths.

Every day, it seems, you get through, just knowing what needs to be said or done without thinking about it. Every day, you seem to mess something up no matter how hard you try, but somehow, the day ends, and you can look back and see how it all worked out. Every day, you look forward with more confidence knowing that you made it through yesterday.

God can make something wonderful from all your goof-ups and from all of your uncomfortable situations.

You may never know how he has used any of it, but you must trust that he was guiding every situation with purpose.

From this you will grow!

> Not only that, but we rejoice in our sufferings, knowing that suffering produces endurance, and endurance produces character, and character produces hope, and hope does not put us to shame, because God's love has been poured into our hearts through the Holy Spirit who has been given to us. (Rom. 5:3–5 ESV)

> And we know that all things work together for good to those who love God, to those who are the called according to his purpose. (Rom. 8:28 NKJV)

The Other Half

If one spouse is caregiving for the other spouse, or if the spouse is an active observer, your communication should be open. Chances are, if a lifetime spouse is involved, that spouse has done very little without the consultation, advice, and support of her mate. I think that might be where the phrase "the other half" comes from. Mom is losing half of who she is. More importantly, she is losing the half that gave her life purpose as she has spent her whole life nurturing and depending on her husband more than anyone, even her children.

Now, although she has their children, pastor, and friends overflowing with competent advice for every situation, the ultimate decisions are hers, or at least it feels like it. How can she easily change from the nurturing, caring, protective confidant to being nurtured, cared for, and protected by those same children? The very children she gave birth to, kissed the boo-boos of, sang lullabies to, and turned back from mistakes made because of bad judgment as adults, are now in control of their lives. Or if you were the perfect child, which is not probable, you still lack the experience to care for them, not to mention you are not in the best situation to give them the attention in which they are accustomed. If she thought all of this, she would be right. Likely, you have no experience caring for the elderly, and if you do, these are *your parents*. We will always have those "hindsight" moments.

Now, it is our responsibility to prove to her we can all work together to make sure both of them are being cared for the best way we know how. We need to make sure we don't have the attitude of "that's just Mom" when we are talking to her. It is likely that Mom knows what she can handle and what she needs help with.

If we take the decision-making away from Mom, then she figures we no longer feel she is competent to make the decisions concerning her or her spouse. If we want to destroy a healthy, functioning human being and turn her into a robot not feeling capable of deciding between a fork or spoon, ink pen or pencil, then take the control of these decisions away from her. We can do our best to reason with her as to the best decisions, but when possible, she should have control of those decisions, which will not have life-or-death consequences. If we don't let her, we will be turning Mom into a fully dependent individual before she needs to be. And we will be destroying her self-reliance, self-esteem, and maybe even what she considers her purpose.

The truth is, each of us has someone we feel is grounded in common sense and practical thinking. You are not likely theirs. It is likely the spouse was that person. You take him away, and she starts questioning the validity in almost everything she does, especially if she isn't used to thinking of God as her ultimate go-to counselor and caregiver.

Our parents need to know we still consider them authority figures, and *they are*. We shouldn't have the attitude they can have what they want if we feel generous or accommodating that particular day. If it is possible for us to do as they request and it doesn't hurt anything, they should have whatever they want within reason. They've worked hard all their lives and made provision for us. It should be our privilege and joy to return their love by still respecting them as our parents.

In fact, unless you take the time to get out of your world and into the world of your parents, you will never be able to comprehend the reality of what is happening within the confines of their existence. They are sucked into an isolated, lonely, forgotten place. This may be the only vaguely secure environment they now know. They are separated from what they consider the world of fresh air, friends, and freedom. Because of their inability to function in that world anymore, they feel forgotten. You may not get it, but someday, you will be in their shoes.

5

Paid Caregivers

Remember when making decisions regarding your parents' care, if you are truly trying to keep them safe and happy, there are no wrong decisions. Sometimes, you have to trust God to take your choices and use them to honor him while you are working to honor your parents. As hard as it is to grasp this fact, sometimes it is plain work to keep them happy and content in a way that will truly reflect an honoring love toward them. God will bless you for this, but even if it doesn't feel as though you are being rewarded for your hard work, remember God put you in this role, and it is your pleasure to live up to the challenge to shine for your God.

At the same time, you, as a caregiver, do have responsibilities to your children, your spouse, and your home; and your parents should understand that. Yet how much of their lives did your parents sacrifice for you? Chances are, you could put much of your wants and rathers on hold for a few years to care for your parents with a loving nonsacrificial attitude. Something very important to remember is not to ever leave their care to someone else. I'm not saying don't have hired caregivers or use the services of a facility, but providing caregivers for your parents should be regarded as a fallback for you, not a replacement. In other words, caregivers didn't grow up with your parents. They wouldn't know their personalities or capabilities, values, or history. *You do!*

Caregivers don't love your parents like you do. Going to see your parents for a few minutes at a time to check in with them and the caregiver is not enough to tell you anything. Your parents may not want to cause more conflict than needed by complaining about things that seem petty. Or they just don't want to make things more complicated, causing friction when life is tough enough already. It could be they have just lost the verbal ability to express a concern. Believe it or not, your parents are more than aware of the burden they are putting on you even when they are in a state that seems ungrateful and belligerent. The truth is, they are miserable over their situation. My goodness, their dispositions change for the same reasons and in the same ways ours do. Who would have thought?!

Communicate with Respect

It is hard when several people are trying to work together but on rotating schedules. Communication is a great big issue and very hard to make happen, but it is a must. One person doesn't need to feel taken advantage of nor does anyone need to be left out of the loop. It may be a good idea to go to a restaurant for a dinner meeting, or to have everyone over to your house once a month to discuss how things are going and to revisit scheduling and new concerns. When I pray, I always try to pray for my actions to honor God. Sometimes, I go away from a situation forgetting that was my goal. Then I have to hold on to the hope that God can use anything I do for his glory. This is how I sleep at night.

Remember to pick your fights. When there are multiple people involved in the caregiving, it is important to remember that if it doesn't hurt anything, it is not worth dissension among the ranks. Your job is to keep check on and to support your fellow caregivers, not to be controlling and domineering. Even if the main caregiving decisions are yours, you can't be there all the time. You are depending on others (maybe many others) to do the majority of hands-on caregiving. It is likely that if you approach your other caregivers with a pigheaded attitude, you will be either ignored or lose some very essential help. On the other hand, being too subservient could lead to losing control of the behavior of the other caregivers.

If you are the sole caregiver, God bless you! It is very important that you find a support system, either within friends, church, or an organized support group. There will be times you need encouragement and confirmation that you are doing the best you can. You also need to be willing to admit you don't have all the answers. When you are looking for your support system, don't choose folks who will patronize you, but women or men who you consider to be wise Christian counselors who will tell you like it is and have some background in which to lend advice.

If you are not a hands-on caregiver, you are not quali-fied to give direction on how to handle routine daily activ-ities and situations. You just don't know what is required to get the objective accomplished. If you are the coordinator and go to caregiver for handling day-to-day events, make sure you have experience with your loved one in any given situation because each event and each person is unique. Often the care receiver reacts better toward a new face or a particular personality. With situations involving dementia or the elderly in general, it is important to do what it takes to accomplish the goal put forth required to maintain their safety or well-being.

Most likely, you know someone who has been in your situation. You may know or have access to professionals who have spent half their lives helping people like you and your loved one. Take advantage of their wise counsel, but be careful to use your own discretion when listening to the answers to questions and talking to others. Talk to multiple friends and professionals and weigh out your choices. Ask for referrals for doctors specializing in medicine specific to your loved one's needs. Don't dismiss counseling. It is hard to keep a clear perspective when you are dealing with this every day and this is your loved one.

Hiring a Caregiver

When interviewing a caregiver for your parents, make sure you know the questions that need to be asked. These questions should be asked and answered specifically. Don't accept vague answers. An experienced caregiver will have questions for you. They will need to know the extent of your loved ones' physical and mental abilities, specifics on routines, and special interest, etc. You want to know she understands your expectations, that she sincerely wants to care for your loved one and is not just looking for a check at the end of the week.

If the caregiver does all the talking during the interview, or says she would never do this or that, she probably doesn't have much experience. In reality, there are so many things you say you would never do, yet you do because it becomes the only way to accomplish a goal. For instance, "I would never tell a half-truth (lie)." So what if a combative dementia care receiver wanted to drive his truck to town? Would you say, "You can't because you don't have the mind to drive," when you are only going to make him angry and mean? Would you say "okay" and hide the keys when you know he will probably spend a few minutes looking for them then go on to something else? It might even make life easier for you if you pretended to help him look for them. Another possibility is for you to "loan" the vehicle out for the afternoon, making him wait for a car that may or may not come back. This is an example I have heard over and over, but it was also a major issue in a personal experience. Driving seems to be one of the first battles when caring for a demented loved one.

Another example would be cooking. Should you continually worry about your loved one burning the house down by forgetting to take something off the stove when another solution could be to cut the power source and pretend the stove isn't working? Maybe your caregiver could have a day they both spend in the kitchen baking and cooking, making memories, and giving your care receiver a sense of value. Your caregiver shouldn't be there to sit. She should be there to engage, entertain, and offer companionship. Otherwise, you would be hiring a sitter, and you only want that if she is sitting with someone unable to have any mental or physical interaction. She should be there to give your loved one a reason to get up in the morning.

I will always remember a sweet day with my mama when I invited her to my house to make muscadine jelly. We made juice, muscadine sauce, and jelly, we cooked down the hulls for fried pies, we caught the stove on fire when the jelly boiled over, but we made a most treasured memory for me. Much of the day she sat in the kitchen in a rocking chair, napping in between giving me instructions, but she was in her element, teaching me how to do something she was no longer able to do on her own. The idea is that she wasn't on her own, and when the jelly on the eye did catch on fire, I was there and it was no big deal. And we had a great day.

The idea of being deceptive and seemingly sinful is hard to justify in the beginning, but your loved one will probably not know the difference, and if the truth would cause an emotional flare-up, the act of deception is kinder. Let's say your parent forgets his spouse has passed away and is constantly waiting and searching for her, are you going to try to calm him by saying, "She is taking care of something she had to do," or are you going to cause him to grieve her loss as if it was the first time he had heard it, along with causing the stress and anxiety of reminding him that his mind is not functioning as it should by saying, "Don't you remember? She passed away. You were there." You may even be blamed for never before telling him.

"Now, we exhort you brethren, warn them that are unruly, comfort the feebleminded, support the weak, be patient toward all men" (1 Thess. 5:14 ESV).

When I first started attending the dementia caregiver support group, someone passed out a piece of paper with this on it: "Today I bent the truth to be kind, and I have no regret, for I am far surer of what is kind than I am of what is true" (Robert Brault). I try not to practice this in general, but for the demented loved one, it is kind, generous, and merciful. (Mr. Brault was kind enough to give me permission to use this quote.)

You may want to use some of these examples when interviewing your caregiver. And you may not approve of my way, but it is important that you and your caregiver are on the same page.

Don't be discouraged. There are good, hired caregivers out there. Take the time and effort to be diligent in the search. Don't expect to find a perfect match the first time. Make sure to check references. Do a background check. Don't take her word for anything. Ask the right questions.

Also, the coordinating family member (or the family) makes the schedule. We know when we need someone there. Be consistent! If we tell her what hours she should be there, we should be prepared for her arrival. Also, we should not constantly be expected to change our schedule for the caregiver. Sure, there are times when it is necessary, but only on rare occasions.

If we want her to clean house, we should tell her exactly what is expected. "I need you to clean the bathrooms, cook and clean the kitchen, vacuum the bedroom, living room, and foyer once a week. You should dust the bedroom and living room once a month." Of course, it is not likely a caregiver will have time to do all of this, or that you would expect it. Just know that light housekeeping will likely mean fix easily prepared meals, put the dishes in the dishwasher or sink, and put the trash in the trash can.

It is important that we spend time with our loved ones when the caregiver is there with them, even staying overnight on occasion. Especially, spend at least three days and nights in the beginning of the new caregiver's trial. I say "trial" because it is not always easy to find just the right caregiver for your loved ones on the first try.

Only in this way can you know what is truly important to your parents for them not to feel as though they are losing their freedom, their independence, let alone their home. Even though they may still be in their home, if they are no longer running the house, it no longer is their home in the sense they are accustomed. They are merely residents in a familiar setting. This is a gut-wrenching experience. At the same time, you want to make sure they are really being cared for just the way you would care for them or even better.

Give the caregiver time to see how you work with and relate to your loved one. She can't successfully get a handle on exactly what is required without being trained and slowly moved into her role. It will give the caregiver an idea of what is expected, what your parents are used to, and avoid uncomfortable situations caused by guessing, and trial and error. If she is a sincere caregiver, she wants to love your parents too.

Listen to your care receivers. They know what they are comfortable with. If you don't know that you can depend on their word, make sure you find the opportunity to be there to check out their concerns.

Monitoring a Caregiver

When checking in with your parents and caregiver, it is very important for you to be in and out with no scheduled arrival times and no common entrance. Be unpredictable, alert, and most of all aware! It gives you the ability to detect areas of concern and to correct problems as they arise. At the same time, you must be very approachable giving the caregiver or care receiver the opportunity to broach his/her concerns.

An example of a problem you might encounter would be when you arrive at bath-time and notice a strong urine smell, knowing this probably should not be an issue, you could assist in the bath and linen changing, using it for a teaching opportunity. It is work to keep the patient, bed, trash can, bedside commode, floor, and surrounding area clean. It also takes good old experience and know how to learn what it takes to maintain a sterile area when you are not accustomed to changing linen sometimes every day or bathing the patient with every diaper change.

Set Guidelines and Define Roles

Make sure the caregiver accepts your guidelines when making purchases, changing the home environment, and deviating from the care receiver's routines. There are times when family members are willing to let a nonfamily care-giver have access to a credit card, which can be convenient for grocery shopping, pharmacy trips, and automobile fuel. It is also helpful if the loved one can shop for things but is no longer capable of handling the purchasing end. Sometimes, it would be nice for them to go on a picnic or make an ice cream run. Just be careful knowing a very ambitious caregiver may decide it is within her power to make day-to-day decisions for your loved one. For instance, if the caregiver has a domineering personality, she may take the opportunity to go clothes shopping for your loved one, leaving the care receiver in the car because it is not her desire to go. If she is doing this, she is not practicing her role as caregiver; she is acting as a personal shopper, which you hadn't invested in. A caregiver would have instead used some ingenuity to find something they could do together to pass the afternoon away.

Some caregivers might get overzealous and decide they can decorate and adjust the living space to accommodate their personal taste at the care receiver's expense. Remember, if you hire an outside caregiver, she should adapt to the comfortable environment of the care receiver, not the other way around. The caregiver may be trying to curb her boredom. If she is that bored, she is probably not engaging your loved one. Ask your parent, or other loved one, if she likes what the caregiver is doing. Approached in the right manner, she will let you know.

Once, I worked with a very domineering caregiver who was given access to the care receiver's credit card. She would get very upset if something happened, and she didn't have that card. I couldn't believe a call I received one day from this caregiver stating that the care receiver's daughter had no business with that card. My question was, if the daughter didn't have any business with that card, who did?! It wasn't like the caregiver needed it for anything. It was just there for an occasional milkshake or other entertainment.

Let's say you have a fairly established caregiver, Dorothy, for your mom. And let's say, there were multiple siblings trying to make the decisions concerning the role of the caregiver. Yet you were the one on hand to make everything run smoothly for them. The rest were all very busy with their own children, businesses, and so forth. It seemed Dorothy was doing a good job in keeping your mom safe and clean, not to mention the fact that she could cook. The only problem was that she seemed to be too controlling. What if Dorothy decided your mom, we will say her name is Sara, needed a new pair of shoes? The one she had was worn out. And you knew Sara had not long before bought the shoes she was wearing. You were even with her when she purchased them. You knew the actual problem was that they were bought for comfort and the overall health of her problem feet, not to be fashionable.

Sara was content with her shoes. Dorothy became so obsessed with getting a new pair of shoes she nagged for months. The reason for the need of shoes eventually changed to the fact that she needed a dressy pair for Easter. Sara would have loved to have dressy shoes, but she didn't want shoes that were painful to wear. In addition, Sara didn't want to go to the store and deal with the whole process of trying on and buying a new pair of shoes when the ones she had were fine.

Dorothy wasn't getting her way, so she started saying the shoes were too heavy on Sara's feet. She nagged until Sara finally told you in front of Dorothy she needed some new shoes. When Dorothy left, Sara said she didn't want to get shoes. Her anxiety level was such that she found it hard to shop in stores. Not wanting to seem stubborn in the fact that Sara didn't need shoes, you asked Sara if she would let a podiatrist check her feet and her shoes. Sara agreed to go. The podiatrist cut her toenails and cleaned up her calluses. The pair of shoes she was wearing was perfect. So you make arrangements for regular maintenance appointments with the podiatrist. Problem solved! Or you would think.

When Dorothy comes back from her day off and finds out what you have done, she is livid. The next time you go over to see how things are going, there is a new pair of shoes sitting on the table. Dorothy seems pleased with her new purchase for Sara because the shoes will go well with the new clothes Dorothy had purchased for her. What was the story behind the new shoes?

When you approach Sara concerning the activities of the day, she carefully tells you the story. Dorothy had coerced her into the car and driven her to the shoe store. There Sara got out of the car, went to the display, picked up a pair of shoes that appeared to be just like the ones she currently wore, other than the color, and walked out, leaving Dorothy to pay. She just wanted Dorothy to leave her alone.

Of course, you would feel bad for Sara having to endure the bullying of the caregiver. And yet you would almost have to laugh because evidently taupe is a dressier, lighter weight, and more comfortable color than black. To Dorothy, she had won the power struggle.

Because Dorothy had the misconception that she had now won, she would be free to go one step further. Dorothy thought she had more expertise than Sara's physical therapist as to the style walker she should use. What arrogance to think herself more qualified than the expert on such an important part of Sara's safety and lifestyle! She actually thought she would be given the authority to decide the style walker above the recommendation of the therapist. What nerve! But she would have to see how far she could go.

Control of the household seemed in her reach. And it all started with being trusted to use the credit card to give Sara a little entertainment on a long wearisome day of dementia and anxiety. All in all, the anxiety would become more prevalent and dread of having to spend the day with this caregiver more intense. Not long after that, Dorothy would be available to find someone else to care for.

Oh yeah, Sara refused to wear those shoes until her son finally talked her into putting them on months after Dorothy had gone. The shoes turned out not to be the same style of shoes she had been wearing. They blistered her feet and made her toes sore. Those shoes would never be mentioned again.

In defense of the siblings providing the caregiver for their mother, they had hired Dorothy to take care of the basic needs of their mom. She did that. She cooked for and bathed Sara; she did the light house cleaning after Sara and herself, and she even did some yard work.

But even in the yard work, Dorothy was changing the yard to be what she felt was more attractive, wanting to spray a whole shrub island with an herbicide. When Sara thought Dorothy had cut the shrubs back to give them a fresh start, she was very pleased, but that shrub island was something Sara was particularly proud of. It represented a lot of work and money invested. She didn't want it to just disappear. The caregiver was so bossy and domineering that it wasn't worth it to fight over this island. She needed someone to do that for her.

To the family, it seemed Sara was being well cared for, and Sara had lost the ability to express her unhappiness because the family was seeing someone diligently working. Seemingly, Sara was only expressing the need for the uninterrupted attention of her children, which wasn't possible for them. To keep her at home, they needed help!

I'm not saying that this lady would not be a suitable caregiver for someone, just not for Sara. If she could find someone with plenty of money who loved to shop and redecorate her house and they shared the same taste, she would be perfect. Sara's caregiver felt she had much better taste than Sara. Initially, Sara tried to work with the caregiver, but she would not listen when Sara expressed her opinion on what she would like when it was decided to tackle a project.

Dorothy was going to make window treatments for Sara's windows. Sara asked for solid blue curtains, but Dorothy thought they should be made from printed material. Sara couldn't bear to confront Dorothy with this, so printed curtains were what she got. Everyone bragged on those window treatments, which undermined Sara's wishes and validated the caregiver's influence over Sara's domain, even those in which she was not hired to manage. Sara lost a little of her confidence and will with every decision Dorothy overrode, leaving Sara feeling defeated.

To Dorothy, Sara was a simple-minded elderly lady who needed someone to develop her palate in décor, both inside and outside the home. Sara was losing ownership of her surroundings. What she had spent years turning into her space was slowly becoming the caregiver's.

On a whole, a caregiver is there when you can't be there. She is there to keep the care receiver content and bring joy to the surroundings along with taking care of your loved one's physical well-being. However, every situation is unique. Listen to the caregiver's suggestions and observations and be willing to approve changes as the situation and disease's progression dictates. Just remember, you and the care receiver decide when changes are necessary.

Look for things that shouldn't be happening if the caregiver is truly being an interactive companion. For instance, if your parent or other loved one has time to get to a neighbor's house before the caregiver notices she is gone, then she may not be engaging her care receiver in activities or conversation. If your parent has time to knock over the Christmas tree, pick it up, move it out of the room, and clean up the mess without help from the caregiver, that caregiver is not doing her job, and probably not on hand to help! If the caregiver has more ailments than your loved one, she probably is not physically capable of looking after your loved one.

If your parent or loved one complains of being left alone at night, you definitely want to research that. Maybe even go sit outside the house to watch. The caregiver may be going outside to smoke or do something even more objectionable, thinking she will not be missed. If you stay involved, you will see the signs.

If you have a caregiver who is quick to tell you by what means and how you should conduct the interest of the household, she may have good intentions, but she doesn't know the history of the family relationships, both sibling and parental. She is not there 24-7, and she has not been there for the last forty or fifty years. Let her talk, listen to her, consider her points, but know in your heart your intentions. Be thankful for her but not obligated to use her opinion as a guide for what you know is right for your family. This is your family and your care receiver's life, and she should feel content and in control of her surroundings if possible, even though the caregiver is responsible for making it work. Also, the caregiver doesn't know the extent of your outside obligations…not really. Communication is the most important aspect of making this work. I don't mean vague suggestions but undeniable instruction.

Hiring a caregiver needs to be a well-thought-out process. She is the employee, and you are the employer. She doesn't become the head of the household. Sure, she has the responsibility to keep your loved ones safe, but it is not her home. She should fit into the care receivers' life and way of living, not the other way around. Changing the care receivers' environment only causes increased anxiety. Although *you* should be careful not to let petty things get under your skin, you should try to distinguish prideful pettiness and legitimate, unsolicited interference.

When you hire a caregiver (your employee), remember that whatever you allow once is setting a precedent for the remainder of her employment. For instance, if you give your employee control over your loved one's schedule and routine, changing comfortable habits, the caregiver could wind up turning the home, which your loved one spent years turning into his sanctuary, into the help's domain. This could leave your loved one in a more dependent and less assured frame of mind. Of course, this makes it easier for the caregiver to control and manipulate her way into the family structure, making it hard for you to have leverage over the household and healthcare decisions, especially if the caregiver has the care receiver intimidated into thinking she doesn't have any say in the decisions being made.

You Are Ultimately Responsible

You are the one ultimately responsible for the care of your loved ones, and you must take care to direct the course of the caregiver's job description. Unless you choose to give the caregiver control of the inner workings of the household and family responsibilities, you must set limits. It is easy for the caregiver to fall in love with the ones she is caring for and to feel the need to get involved in things that are not her concern. You might want to be best friends with the caregiver, but it can make for some uncomfortable situations when you don't agree with what is best for your mom or dad. Trying to befriend the caregiver may cause problems. An aggressive caregiver may decide she is more qualified than you to care for your loved one, nullifying your decisions. She may actually be, but that is for you to discern.

If you are not prepared to become the authoritative figure in a parent-child relationship, it can be easy to leave the hard decisions to someone else. By doing this, you are opening a mountain of issues. Your parent would become totally dependent on the caregiver. Your employee could become your parent's confidant and make your loved one second-guess any decision or change you may want to make. You may find yourself in a position to be the humble subordinate in your parent's life. If the caregiver's control includes money or a charge card, even if she uses it for what she maintains is the good of your parent, you may eventually find yourself sucked into a situation where it is hard to say no. She could use it as a source of power and manipulation. Not that she would, but she could.

These are just a few examples of what to look for; there are more.

Yes, it is hard to find qualified help, but it is out there, so don't be afraid to set the caregiver straight right away because the interference could grow to become a major problem.

You also have to be considerate in that the caregiver is leaving his home environment and taking on someone else's totally foreign atmosphere and space. Your loved one is not the only one having to make adjustments, so is the caregiver. There will be challenges for both of them. Stay in there and stay aware! You don't want someone unless he shows the desire to really love and care for the well-being of the one needing the care, but you do want to make the caregiver as comfortable as possible.

The main thing is to look for experience, sincerity, humbleness, and a compassionate heart in your caregiver. A sense of humor is a great asset in every caregiving situation. Whenever a caregiver can make my mama chuckle, that caregiver has my heart. What is more important than someone sincerely bringing joy to my parent's confused and sometimes seemingly insecure surroundings!

He or she is out there, but it takes time and patience to find yours.

Respect the Caregiver

Whether you hire a caregiver or have a volunteer, take extra care to do special little things for him to show that he is a valuable part of the team. At this point, you are, like it or not, dependent on him to be everything you can't be or don't want to be. Take time to take out the trash, clean a toilet, sweep the carport, and cut the grass on his days off. These chores are not his priority if the primary agreement is care for your parents. For the most part, that is a full-time job of its own if either parent is debilitated. If it is hard for you to keep up when you are there, it is hard for him as well. The work shouldn't build up to make his first day back a catch-up day. This way, you let him know that you know he has a big job and that you appreciate his care for your parents. You love your parents or you wouldn't be doing this, so step up and make their surroundings clean, bright, and pleasant just like they would have it for you. Of course, you may have the attitude, "I don't do all this at home." Well, this is not your home. You know what your parents expect for their home to feel right. You also know what will make the caregiver feel comfortable. Make them comfortable in their surroundings.

When there is an occasion where you and your family come over to eat or spend the day, remember to leave the house in the same order and cleanliness to which you found it. Take out the trash, sweep, mop, or vacuum the floor, wash and put up the dishes, and put the furniture back in place. You may not be used to doing this because your parents have always been able to take care of the cleanup, and you may have never even considered the fact that someone had to do it. It was something taken for granted. You can no longer do this. Your caregiver, whether volunteer or paid, has plenty to do as a caregiver without the added work of cleaning up after you. Not to do this is disrespectful to the caregiver and your parents.

If your parents are not capable of looking after their home, you are certainly leaving the message that their well-being and comfort are not your responsibility nor of your concern. When you decided to keep your loved one in their home and to see that they were cared for, it also became your responsibility to maintain their home. If you can't do your part to keep them in a clean and comfortable environment where they can be proud of their home, then hire someone who will do a great job of cleaning.

Don't leave it to the good-natured friend or caregiver. That doesn't shine a bright light on your character, although no one would probably know except those picking up your slack and your parents. This doesn't leave a message of "It is my joy to care for you." And the fact is, hiring a housekeeper leaves you available to spend extra time loving on your parents, something that no one else can do like you. That would make the money spent on a housekeeper well worth the dollar.

Joy in Serving

The joy you will find in serving and loving on these very special people is not the same joy you have when you find yourself planning your wedding, or when your children are born, or when you land your first real job. It is not the same joy you feel when your son kicks his first field goal, or your daughter graduates from high school, or has her first child. It is the joy of times past, times shared with these loved ones knowing you can't go back, but loving the reflection of those long-ago days of sunshine and rainbows, of lightning bugs and butterflies. Stories to be told, lessons that were learned, and the joy of having shared these treasured memories with the most special loved ones in your life is what this time is about, holding on to them for the time being because that is what you have, the time being.

God is always with you and knows where your heart is. He has got this! Keep your heart in touch with the reality of what is happening. Know what you can do without feeling overwhelmed and trust God. You are only one person, but God is everything. He's got your back. Pray for his will to be done.

There were many times when I *know* God had Mr. Robertson's back, but there was one particular time that found me running to do—I had no idea what, but I ran. This is the way it went down. Mr. and Mrs. Robertson were sitting in the swing outside. We had just finished eating a leisurely picnic lunch. They had settled down in a swing enjoying the sunshine when I started moving the dishes and food back inside. As far as I knew, they were not even thinking of doing more than swinging the hour away.

I didn't think I had been gone long enough for them to have done anything. And yet, there he was trying to pull up an empty piece of landscape fabric originally used to hold potted transplants, keeping them free of weeds and mud. I think the cloth was about twelve-by-twenty feet. I really have no idea of the size, but it was pretty long and wide.

Anyway, he had one side loose and was trying to pull the remainder free from the stakes when the wind blew under the fabric and swept him up on his tiptoes a couple of times, each time easing him back down solidly to the ground. Thankfully, he held on tight. The third time the wind swooped under the cloth, it raised him up, and then, as pretty as you please, it slowly lowered him gently, laying him on his back. It was as if angels had been supporting him as he eased down. Boy, was I holding my breath! I arrived just in time to help him back on his feet. God is everything and everywhere you can't be!

Whatever you choose to do, take heart in these verses.

> Count it all joy, my brothers, when you meet trials of various kinds, for you know that the testing of your faith produces steadfastness. And let steadfastness have its full effect, that you may be perfect and complete, lacking in nothing. If any of you lacks wisdom, let him ask God, who gives generously to all without reproach, and it will be given him. But let him ask in faith, with no doubting, for the one who doubts is like a wave of the sea that is driven and tossed by the wind. (James 1:2–6 ESV)

Do not be anxious about anything, but in everything by prayer and supplication with thanksgiving let your requests be made known to God. And the peace of God, which surpasses all understanding, will guard your hearts and your minds in Christ Jesus. (Phil. 4:6–7 ESV)

Caregiver Perspective/Common Feelings

When you are a primary caregiver and are there routinely, day in and day out, it seems like a lifetime. It seems as if you are the one whose life is on hold while the others seem unaware and unconcerned with the lives up the hill or around the corner so to speak. Sometimes, it seems as if it is you and the loved one in a vacuum separated from the rest of the world. You have to know, that is part of your job. Do your best to make it easy for the family to come and visit without the guilt of not being there all the time. Just like you, the family needs breathing space where the wearisome responsibility of their loved ones and the everyday pressures and hardships of life can be worry-free for a while. The family members have to have time to reflect on how to best be there, and you are the one they have trusted to love their parents when they are not there. Heed the family's instructions and care for the loved ones as if you were their child, but remember you are the employee and are there to carry out the job as agreed on at hiring. Over time, these things may change, but only at the family's initiation.

Common Feelings for All

Whether you realize it or not, you will get attached to the ones you are caring for, and you will feel like they need you, and you are the only one who can care for them in a way that will make them comfortable. You are the one they can really count on to keep them safe and content but give someone else a chance because your energy and time are expendable.

The ones you are caring for need you, but you need to keep your identity and life outside of caregiving. For this reason, you may find your role as the main caregiver is not necessary anymore. Your role may change, and that is okay because there is still more to be done than you have the time or energy to do. It is all important. Remember, all you do is to be done as though it is being done unto the Lord. Every job is important, and every job is appreciated, though not always acknowledged. Maybe you feel taken for granted but take a week off and see what doesn't get done. I warn you, there will be a lot of catching up. You just don't realize. The others may not realize it, but everyone finds out.

"Footsteps of Jesus"—what a song! I grew up singing this hymn many a Sunday morning at our little country church in Jackson, Georgia. It has never meant more to me than it does during this time in my life. No matter where those footsteps lead, whether it is the pathway of serving, living life just trying to rake out a livable income, or trying to find security in his mercy and direction as our parents continue life's journey into their final years, it is important to follow the footsteps of Jesus.

Be Patient

Be Present in Today

The most important thing to remember as you begin this journey is that you don't need to worry today about what may become the future. What seems impossible to manage today will become routine or no longer an issue tomorrow. In the beginning, it is hard to figure out what is going on. Just take your time, be on hand, and expect only what you see. Don't make excuses and don't jump to conclusions. Whatever it is, God has you there, and you are privileged to have this opportunity to show love to your loved ones.

Of course, there are those times when your parents may seem to take advantage of your sincere effort to care for them. But be careful. You definitely want to make sure they are being manipulative and really don't need something. If manipulation is the case, maybe you could find an alternative solution to what they want. It is most likely they only want your time and attention. In that case, maybe you could hire a companion for them or take them to visit a friend or relative. Maybe, it would suffice to mark on a calendar the times you could spend with them as long as you were consistent in keeping those promised times.

When you visit, show them your undivided, loving, and caring attention. Your total focus should be on them. Make sure they never get a sense of your desire to be somewhere else doing something else. And don't sit and doze, watch TV, play games, or talk on your phone. This is their time with you! God blessed you with them from the time you were conceived, and he is blessing and growing you as you care for them now.

Be patient. As God is growing you, so is he preparing them for their homecoming. Although it feels like your life is being disrupted and you are being inconvenienced, God has enriched your very being by giving you the opportunity to pray and care for the well-being, both physically and spiritually, of your parents.

Alert to All Needs: Emotional, Physical, Mental, Spiritual

Listen to your parents! Be sensitive to their needs. Whatever you do, don't assume they are making big deals over nothing when they voice a concern. If they have a concern, then it is legitimate, and you should investigate. What if you felt uneasy about something and everyone blew you off! Well, that is what you would be doing to them. Remember, they are the very people who sat up with you at night to ward off the boogeyman. Yes, you were a child, but nonetheless, their fears are just as real as yours were then. The only thing is their fears are about a real-life boogeyman creeping up behind them. And this monster is going to get closer and closer until it catches up. But before it consumes its victims, it stalks and watches while carefully planning a strategy to knock its targets right off their feet. Granted, you can't and shouldn't put your whole life on hold but try to figure out how to curb your loved ones' anxiety with an attitude of love and compassion for what they are experiencing.

Environment

Make sure your parent's environment stays consistent. Even a small change of routine can take away the feeling of being at home. For instance, doing away with their nightly coffee before bed, or morning coffee before the house wakes up to a bustling new day, can give them a feeling of loss. Changing the thermostat seems like such a minor issue, but if your mom and dad are used to their house being 83 degrees Fahrenheit, then 75 degrees takes away the comforting, secure feeling of their home. Older folks seem to need a warmer room temperature for some reason.

Next, the furniture needs to remain where they put it. If you must move or change the furnishings, let them be a part of the move. This is their home. They need to have a say so.

You should prepare the types of food they are used to eating. I'm not saying don't try to give them a healthy diet. You can always tweak the menus, but don't take the joy out of their mealtime.

Remember, your parents still need a sense of control and satisfaction in doing some things for themselves without someone else's permission. It might be something as simple as sneaking a candy bar during the middle of the afternoon or sneaking a Coke in the middle of the night. Let them have this special time to *reward themselves* for another day accomplished. Or give them this time to enjoy a quiet, relaxing moment winding down by themselves after the rest of the house has retired. Especially afford them this time if the candy bar or Coke is a small one, and there are no health issues involved.

Offering a candy bar as a reward for eating their dinner is not the same as sneaking it. What had been a means of satisfaction now has a demeaning connotation. They are not children! They need the control of deciding when they get to treat themselves.

They have spent a lifetime establishing routines and habits. Why should we feel obligated to take these away from them? Why can't we find ways of making these habits and routines possible? For instance, if the chair at the dining room table is not the safest for them to sit in, maybe instead of making them move positions at the table, we could just switch chairs.

All these small, seemingly insignificant details mean the difference of being home or being somewhere totally alien, of keeping their dignity or being belittled. Of course, you should listen to the care receiver's opinions and suggestions and then determine what is important. Follow their lead. But always make your parents' comfort a priority.

"Honor your father and mother" (this is the first commandment with a promise) (Eph. 6:2 ESV).

Anxiety

I don't think there is a doctor anywhere who would say extreme anxiety is something you can tell someone he just needs to get over or deal with, especially with the elderly who have so many obstacles contributing to it. Anytime you can avoid a situation that can contribute to the onset of an anxiety attack, that trigger should be extracted from the equation. This would include social situations, financial decisions, family issues, fear of storms, and controversial people—any kind of situation that requires expectations beyond day-to-day routine. To recognize these anxiety triggers and not do everything possible to avoid them is to simply show a lack of compassion.

This is easier said than done. You shouldn't have to deny them those things that bring joy to their lives, but you can take measures not to expose your loved one to those things known to cause anxiety. For instance, if you are having a Christmas party and you feel they would love to be a part of it yet wouldn't be able to deal with the activity or crowd of people for an extended time, put a time limit on it. Or maybe, it would be better to have a few visitors at a time. It could be that having an "adult party only" with the children visiting another time would make it easier for your parents. Or maybe, having the party during a time of the day when your parents are at their best—for instance, midmorning for brunch.

Listen

If your parent says he is trying but doesn't show any effort, know that if during his cognitive years he worked hard and showed impeccable integrity, he is trying. His brain just isn't sending the message to the rest of his body or he is just so tired he doesn't have the strength to move. Imagine standing in the middle of thirty to fifty thousand moving, chirping chicks while watering, feeding, keeping them warm, and weeding out the sick and dead every day. That's what my in-laws did. It was work, and they never shrugged off a day of giving these chicks the best care, not to mention keeping up with all the other everyday chores of farming. So if they say they can't do something, I believe them.

Whenever discussing an issue with your parent, as long as you don't know what is right and what is wrong, assume he is telling it like it is, and then do what it takes to research the matter. The first place to start is his level of anxiety. Of course, the anxiety may be the cause of the problem, but it could also be the result of it. This is going to take time, patience, and sometimes confrontation with other caregivers, but remember "no one better mess with my mama and daddy." Don't take the explanation of the one causing or seemingly causing conflict; of course, she will not see reason for concern.

My mother-in-law is deathly afraid of thunderstorms. Whenever a thundercloud comes up, she goes in the house, unplugs all the appliances, closes all the doors and windows (even the inside doors), and turns out the lights. It would be totally insensitive for a caregiver to, in Mrs. Robertson's state of anxiety and fear, open the doors, turn on the television, and light up the room, knowing that she would be terrified. She has spent a lifetime being afraid of bad weather. It is not likely that she is going to be convinced that there is nothing to be afraid of now. Even though it may seem that she takes her fear to a silly extreme, to her, the fear is real. To her, the caregiver is purposefully putting her and the caregiver in danger.

We say our parents cared for us and loved us, and now, it is our turn and our pleasure to care for them. Do we really mean it? Will we find joy in it? We can do nothing God can't bless! Search your true motive and intentions, which should always be caring for your parents. Your heart is going to guide your actions. There are many ways to care for someone, and none is less loving than the other as long as you do it with a pure heart, knowing what is best for you and your loved one. So guard your heart with all care.

"Keep thy heart with all diligence; for out of it are the issues of life" (Prov. 4:23 KJV).

Physical

Folks who come to visit my in-laws are always commenting on how sweet they are just sitting on the couch, holding hands and quite often exchanging sweet kisses. My father-in-law used to take long walks outside with my mother-in-law and me, but now he does well to make it to the bathroom and table for meals. Some days he communicates clearly and needs very little help. Other days, he needs assistance doing everything. You have to be open to the immeasurable possibilities as God shines the morning sun to the scene he has directed for that particular day.

Soon you begin to recognize most days as familiar, maybe not experienced every day, but no longer a disappointment or a surprise. Of course, there is always the uncertainty of how much he should be doing and what he should be discouraged from doing. Do you hinder him and make him frustrated and unhappy, or do you let him try to do what he wants and just make it as safe as possible?

What is the worst that could happen?! This is a very important concept! You don't want him to fall or aspirate, but these things might happen no matter how many precautions you take. This is why you should not take away the things he finds joy in. Let him do those things that make life bearable but let him do them in the safest manner possible—just let him do them "leaning on the everlasting arms." Know nothing can happen that is not God's will.

"The eternal God is your dwelling place, and underneath are the everlasting arms. And he thrust out the enemy before you and said, Destroy" (Deut. 33:27 ESV).

Spiritual

Visitors tell my mother-in-law, "God is here for you, trust him to care for Mr. Robertson."

To this, she replies, "God can't be there for everyone." She says this because she doesn't feel cared for by God because she wasn't prepared for anything like what is happening to them. Deep down, she knows God is there and that God takes care of everyone. But sometimes, when he grows us in faith and love, it hurts. We can have peace if we trust in our God. It is easy to say this when it is not happening to you. That is why it is imperative for you to take time to start conditioning your heart now before you are the one lost in grief, not feeling cared for by a God you have acknowledged your undying devotion. It can happen!

My mother-in-law is a very devoted Christian woman. She reads devotional books all the time, trying to find the comfort and peace she knows she should feel. In fact, she is working on five different ones searching for hope and praying for his care. Yet what she sees as she lays the books down is a man with a very ugly disease deteriorating right before her eyes, making her feel forgotten by God. She knows God is there, but she hurts right down in her gut, making her feel like someone is physically turning her inside out while she is battling with everything that makes her who she is.

7

And Now, Why, God?
It Happened to Her/Him

Therefore, since we have been justified by faith, we have peace with God through our Lord Jesus Christ. Through him we have also obtained access by faith into this grace in which we stand, and we rejoice in hope of the glory of God. More than that, we rejoice in our suffering, knowing that suffering produces endurance, and endurance produces character, and character produces hope and hope does not put us to shame, because God's love has been poured into our hearts through the Holy Spirit who has been given to us. (Rom. 5:1–5 ESV)

If there is one thing I pray for myself and the reader, it is that when we reach this time in our lives, we will remember the love and care that God provides for us and that we will depend on the hope we have in Jesus.

While Jesus was on the cross experiencing the most excruciating torture imaginable, he was taking care of his mother by giving her John to provide for her and love her as only a son could. Jesus took care of his mother; we can surely look after our parents with the same heart and understanding for their needs.

Respect

If the elderly person needing care was "Sir" to you before the disease advanced in severity, he is still "Sir," not "buddy," "sweetie," or "fellow." You pay the same respect to that person as you did before. He has seen more than you, experienced more life than you, and has overcome more than you. Of course, if you have had a "buddy"-type relationship, then that is right for you.

Remember all those things that make the person who he is still exist and not deep down inside but right there at the surface where he feels. He understands he has a handicap that prevents him from being understood or considered capable of comprehending his needs or the spoken word when he is the topic of conversation. He understands a lot more than you think, and talking about his impairments in front of him is just as rude as it would have been before dementia set in.

He can communicate the way he feels, and he will, but not on terms that seem logical to us, but by expressing his misery as it builds from frustration and determination not to be gotten the best of. It sounds cut and dry, but it is not because, how do you control the frustrated misbehavior, warranted or not? The only thing I know is that God has it, and the situations should be handled with patience, love, and the respect and honor God requires.

Some Lessons Learned

Sometimes, there is much of the past that must be dealt within the caregiver and care receiver's history. Many times, it is just too late to take care of it before the caregiving begins. You need to come to terms with it, and from this point forward, start a new relationship. Sometimes, that relationship becomes closer and more loving as the care receiver becomes more dependent on you and you prove your dedication, persistence, and dependability toward him. Other times, the very person who thought you hung the moon finds it hard to even be in the same room with you anymore. In both cases, you need to love him and respect him, knowing that deep down, he thinks you are the reason the sun shines. He loves you, he hates the disease, and whether he admits it or not, he knows something is wrong. Often, we hurt the ones who are the closest or the ones who seem to be able to withstand the hurt the most.

To keep things in perspective, you need to remember to laugh when it is warranted. Believe me, there are times that definitely call for a good belly jiggler. Sure, dementia is a very sad and difficult disease to live with, but through this, God incorporates humor, which should definitely be recognized and put into our long-term memory banks.

Maybe a night when you are trying to sleep, but your mind won't shut down the day's events, you can enjoy with peace the day's comic antics.

I can tell you some doozies from my own experience. Of course, at the time, there was a little frustration included. So here goes my first story. I love this story because I think it defines the course of a demented day. Here goes: I drive up to my in-laws' home on the farm where three chickens have escaped their pasture. My mother-in-law is outside, slinging a pan of water and then picking up a broom, furiously scrubbing the cement walk leading to the front door while under her breath declaring the fate of the fowl who indiscriminately left its droppings at her door. In the meantime, my father-in-law, who is a moderate fall risk, is in the yard, crouched down with both arms stretched out running this way and that, playing a very enthusiastic game of "Catch Me if You Can" with the chickens. A more comic scene you have never witnessed. Although I try my best to divert their energies, my efforts are to no avail. So I sit down and wait for the scene to play itself out. It does, and none for the worse. I still enjoy sharing that story.

As a side note, my father-in-law didn't catch anything except a nap that day. And because he wouldn't allow his son nor my son in his yard, they searched at night after the household had long been dreaming looking for those chickens' roosts. It took about a week, but alas, all was calm again.

Next, we have the story of the gully folly. After lunch each day, they enjoyed getting out in the yard and cleaning up fallen tree limbs, raking the leaves, or just taking a leisurely walk around the farm. Well, more and more often, my father-in-law would take off on his own. His having dementia made it necessary for me to follow close enough to intervene had I needed to—hiding behind cars, bushes, and trees—staying far enough away to keep him from knowing I was there. Of course, it didn't take long for him to get wise to me. Therefore, he learned to walk a few steps, stop, turn his head just enough to see where I was and continue on. I know he truly had eyes in the back of his head because there is no way he could have known for sure where I was.

Well, one day he got away from me, and when I noticed he was gone, he was at a distance that left me no time to play my cat-and-mouse game. He would have made it to the road before I could have stopped him. This time, he surely saw me and took off, but not toward the road. He found a way to put a gully between us. What could I do? I couldn't think of anything other than going around. Once he saw me coming, I expected him to take off again, but with no adieu, he turned and headed into the ditch.

Getting down there wasn't a problem; he just sort of half ran, half slid. The problem was how to get up the other side. He would back up as far as he could, get a running start, and with all his might, take that bank. He would get halfway up, stop, and with no other choice, head backward once again to the bottom of this large ditch padded with blackberries and greenbrier. Well, at this point, I knew I could only watch. So helplessly, and thankful that my mother-in-law was still at the house, I watched him do this maybe four times before on his way down, he lost his footing and, just as easy as you please, laid down on top of the sticky vines. Luckily, not where there were any seriously exposed thorns. Well, thanking God that the fall had been uneventful, and that until he got good and ready to have me help him up, he was safe. I tried a couple of times, but he just crossed his arms over his chest and told me to keep my hands off him.

As I said earlier, my mother-in-law had not yet realized we were gone. But as fate would have it, my phone rang. I told her we were down the driveway, and everything was fine. Then, as an invitation to come check on us, I told her she could just stay at the house, and we would be back soon. Here she came like a bloodhound sniffing her way to her mark, as if she instinctively knew something was going on. When she saw him, panic immediately set in, and all my efforts to tell her he was fine were useless. I told her I was just letting him decide when he was ready to get up. She couldn't stand to see him like that. She immediately called for her grandson to come help. She told him we couldn't get him up. Now, the last thing we needed was more excited people on the scene, trying to take charge.

So before help arrived, I picked him up and helped him keep his balance as he climbed out of the ditch on the side he previously ran down. Thankfully, I think he knew he was in for an unpleasant event had he resisted any longer. Also, the longer he stayed in that ditch, the more exposed he was to those precocious thorns. On the way up, he mumbled, "What are you going to do with me now?"

I told him he could do whatever he liked, but we would do it together. I will always remember his trying to get up the other side of the gully and how I could reason to leave him alone because the vines and the shape of the ditch made it unlikely that no more than his pride would be worse for the wear. Besides that, for the life of me, I couldn't think of anything I could do. You could see God's premeditated plan as he brought nature together to form that ditch for that occasion.

Go to God

Eventually, we are going to find ourselves in the same predicament as our loved ones are now. Growing old. Needing help. So we should take heed, absorb what is happening, and prepare our own minds, attitudes, and emotions. Someday, we are going to find ourselves in a fish tank, gasping for air.

We are to live our lives trusting God to provide the right path for us. We may be given the opportunity to rest in his love and embrace while suffering the pain and sickness of cancer, the awful lostness of dementia, Parkinson's, heart disease, or just the feebleness of aging. But God will provide the path needed to lead us to him. Our responsibility is to live with the intention of honoring God no matter what he uses to grow us. As we live in his love, God brings those we interact with closer to him.

This is a very scary concept for me because I have seen the effect of all these diseases on the families and the individuals living these heartbreaking struggles. I don't know if I have what it will take, but I know this is what God intends. It is how I want to feel, and I pray that I have what it will take to be able to cope. I also know I want to be a tool God uses to bring eternal salvation to my loved ones. I just don't know I have what it takes!

No temptation has overtaken you that is not common to man. God is faithful, and he will not let you be tempted beyond your ability, but with the temptation he will also provide the way of escape, that you may be able to endure it. (1 Cor. 10:13 ESV)

Trust in the Lord with all your heart, and do not lean on your own understanding. In all your ways acknowledge him, and he will make straight your paths. (Prov. 3:5–6 ESV)

I know these verses, but somehow, I also know the strength to live them out is going to have to be supernatural. I'm praying ahead for divine intervention.

I do know that there are people who intentionally live out these verses. Aunt Maggielene, who struggled with Parkinson's, was my amazing example of carrying faith and trust in God's total provision into her final days. Here is just one example: After a very traumatic fall, she told me that that fall was part of God's plan. Later one night, when she was feeling anxious and unsettled just days before she saw the Lord face-to-face, she focused on the ceiling in the corner of the room from where she lay and counted her blessings from the Lord. How honored I felt watching this lady live out her heart during one of the hardest nights of her life!

Oh give thanks to the Lord; call upon his name; make known his deeds among the peoples! Sing to him, sing praises to him; tell of all his wondrous works! Glory in his holy name; let the hearts of those who seek the LORD rejoice! Seek the LORD and his strength; seek his presence continually! (Ps. 105:1–4 ESV)

Support Group: Learn from Others

My support group has been very helpful to me. It is amazing to listen to these very sincere loved ones tell their stories, many times with tears in their eyes knowing their hearts are breaking, and then see someone else who has been there tell her story with laughter because coming out of it you can put it all in perspective. Or see the whole room cry in sympathy for all a fellow caregiver's grief from the loss of the person she had promised to love, honor, and obey till death they do part. The person she is caring for doesn't even resemble that man. The tissues make their round and the bond of these very strong people is wound tighter. God bless these most precious friends.

The following are letters between myself and one of these friends. While listening to my friend tell of her care for her husband and how blessed she would feel if her stepchildren would lend her a hand in his care, I felt I might be able to shed a little light their way. I thought that once their eyes were opened to what she was experiencing day in and day out, they might step up and help. He was their dad! While the letter never landed in the hands of the husband's children, it meant the world to my friend knowing she had support and love from someone who understood.

May 1, 2016
Dear _____

My name is Martha Robertson, and I belong to the caregiver support group your stepmother so faithfully attends. I am writing to let you know how much she has meant to me. Her faithfulness to your father is an inspiration to all of us in the group. Her devotion to your father truly reflects her love and adoration for him. God has surely proven his love for him through the provision of your stepmother as your dad's caregiver during the neediest time in his life.

I know it is very hard for you having to watch as his health declines. I know because I watched both of my parents as they lived out the last seasons of their earthly lives. It was one of the hardest things I ever had to do.

I know Janie is facing the hardest days of her life because I can see it in her face— the tired, drawn look of someone who is fighting a long, impossible battle. Her eyes show the weariness of her days and the sleepless nights that never seem to end. Right now, she needs a reprieve so she can gain her bearings for the weeks and months to come. I know your lives are so full, but her heart and emotions are so, so overflowing with the need to share with someone who is as much in love with your dad as she. God has been so good to all of you. I know Janie has felt blessed by your dad, and I know your dad has been blessed by the loving, caring heart of your stepmother.

Janie is such a beautiful name. It means to be a benevolent, inspirational, determined, and courageous person. It means she is a gift from God.

I write this letter just to let you know; although we think she is Wonder Woman, she could really use any help you can offer. She is tired, and these are the days God has set for all of you to come together and love on each other knowing that family is first and foremost important in your lives and your relationship with God. There is nothing forever besides family and God. You can't change these two entities, but you can pour your love into them.

Sincerely and with much compassion,
Martha Robertson

May 3, 2016
Dear Martha,

I am truly overwhelmed by the loving and kind letter you wrote for my stepchildren. It is amazing to me what a wonderful person you are to do such a sweet thing.

Yes, you can certainly understand the struggle all of us are facing. Some days we don't even want to get out of bed. But we do, and we get done what needs to be done. Just from your letter, it is obvious you are one of the most compassionate and loving caregivers ever.

Your letter, although very sweet and gentle, is something my stepchildren will never see. Saying that, please know it touched me in the most wonderful way possible to know someone out there cares enough to write it. The letter may have been for them, but it gave me more strength than I have felt for a long time. To say "thank you" does not even cover my appreciation.

We are both tired from all we do, and we have a long way to go. Thank goodness for our group, and especially thank goodness for lovely people like you. It's thoughtful gestures like your letter that make the world a better place. I thank God for you and that we have our group to help us through.

God bless you, sweet lady,
Janie

The following is a letter to my friends in the support group after a very emotional hour and a half of the group embracing a newcomer who was so overwhelmed by the inevitable future she was going to have to face for what could be years.

Dear friends,

As I sat and listened to your stories today, I was touched by the love that was exuding from the room. They say soldiers going into battle return home with brothers much closer than siblings. They have become family in a whole other sense. They found out literally what it means to be dependent on their fellow warriors for their every breath. Sometimes that breath is very shallow, almost undetectable. But without those brothers, they would be lost to life, or worse sanity.

I think of the battle you are all in, what a tremendous outfit you are equipped with. God bless each of you for coming and sharing your life. I think of your devotion to your loved one and your determination to make the right decisions to care for him or her. Just that you were there, hands on, loving the person and caring for that person without even questioning the fact that you are the one who belongs there reveals the love that has cemented your lives. Whether you are caring for your parents or a spouse, the years past have meant enough to you that you are taking this journey at their side, carrying their weight while struggling to remember who they really are. Your love is so apparent. It has to be a tremendous love because I know it is a tremendous load.

There is no joy in the work you have to do; the joy must come from the days that grew and deepened the respect and love you have treasured from days gone by. I don't know where you find it, but I know that if there weren't some form of joy, you couldn't do it. I would love to see scrapbooks containing the memories of your lives well lived. The dreams you shared coming true even though at the time they weren't exactly what you had in mind. God provided so well, and now he has put before you the hardest thing you will ever have to do. God can only provide you with his word, friends, and, if you are lucky, family to support you.

The Lord is my strength and my shield; in him my heart trusts, and I am helped. (Ps. 28:7 ESV)

I pray for each of you asking God to give you peace and fortitude because you need it if anyone ever did. Thank you for including me in your group. It is humbling to me to have such strong people for examples.

Love,
Martha

Conclusion

One Last Thought

It's true, you can't do this by yourself. You have to ask for help. You have to be purposeful. You have to be cautious. You have to be humble. You have to be prepared. You have to be steadfast. You have to be willing to be faithful in the knowledge that you are doing the best you can and let God take that and work his perfect will through it.

The tears are good, the grief is good, and the acceptance is good. The prayers and petitions are good. Feeling your weakness is good. Feeling God's embrace, strength, and peace is how you manage each day.

If you have someone you are caring for and you are stepping up to love them into this final chapter, making it okay for them to be whom they have become knowing it wasn't their choice, you are my hero, you are their hero, and you are God's workman.

It is the hardest, most hurtful, most tiring, most rewarding job there is. Accept it, and as God leads you, find each day rewarding.

You can do it, but you can't do it without help, lots and lots of help, along with God's guidance and comfort.

At night, may your last words be "God, thank you for being with me today, and, Lord, please carry me through tomorrow knowing I am following you each step of the way. May your will be done and my faith remain strong. In Jesus's name, amen."

Keeping these things in mind and remembering that your care receiver really does love you no matter how hard he makes it for you, when the time comes, you will be able to say, "We did it." You will be able to say it just as my cousin did when she saw God remove the need for her family to care for her in-laws any longer.

You made sure they were protected, loved, cared for, enjoyed, and prayed over all the way until God decided it was time for him to be their all-exclusive caregiver.

God raised you up to do a very specific job, then he said, "You have done what I set apart for you to do. Now, let me take it from here."

When God takes over the whole of the caregiving, you will still need to rely on God to fill your days and mind on a new season in your life. Your whole caregiving season has been focused on your loved one, and then it goes away just like that (a snap of the fingers). Now, it is time to find new satisfying adventures! The God who fought with you in the trenches of caregiving is by your side during the lonesome time you will experience working your way into a new direction and hopefully loads of adventure. Look for ways to keep your life rewarding. They are there. You just have to jump at the opportunities to fly again.

God bless you!

A Daughter's Prayer for Her Parents
Martha Robertson

Lord, thank you for my blessings,
Gifts to me from you.
Help me use these blessings
To live my life in truth.
Help me learn to guide my heart
In a path not led to stray
But a path that leads to you, Lord,
Not turning from your way.
Help me each and every day
To rely on you.
Help me know right from wrong,
And recognize the truth.
Thank you for sending me
Christian soldiers who
Encourage, lift up,
And turn me back to you.
Father, I pray your will will find
Its way through all I do
And all I have done.
My intention has been to glorify your son.
Lord, you've blessed me
With a family to shine for you.
For this blessing, I pray this song to you.
Bless my parents everyday
Help me encourage them to pray.
Open their eyes that they might see
Answered prayers straight from thee.
Bless my parents with joyful hearts,

Feeling your touch from each new day's
    start.
Keep their thoughts both fresh and aware
That you will embrace them and show that
    you care.
Father, I pray your will be done
as I humbly bow in the name of your son.

The Picture on the Wall
Martha Robertson

Like the picture on the wall,
Tells the story in its all,
The path whose destination is sure,
Yet, hides its lot as lessons endured.
Lined with stories true and real,
The kind your heart absorbs and feels.
Tales of a past and promises of days to
    come,
Hidden by the mist of the early morning
    sun.
The mist that holds the wonders of
    tomorrow,
That promises happiness, adventure, and
    sorrow.
Beyond the mist he has made known to
    her the path of life.
Leaving her legacy to those whose wings
    she set in flight,
Back, now, to care for her as she prepares
    to leave this life of worry and of fear,
To find joy in the presence of the Lord she
    finds so wonderfully dear.

"You will show me the path of life; In your presence is fullness of joy; At your right hand are pleasures forever-more" (Ps. 16:11 NKJ).

ABOUT THE AUTHOR

Martha spent her first five years on a farm in Stockbridge, Georgia. Later, her family moved to the country in Butts County, Georgia, where she graduated from Jackson High School. She studied at Abraham Baldwin Agricultural College in south Georgia and received her BSA with a major in horticulture from UGA.

While working at a greenhouse/nursery in Coweta County, Georgia, Martha met and married Tony. They had two sons, at which time she transitioned into the role of a stay-at-home mom, home schooling, being active in church, and the county's 4-H program.

Once their children graduated from school, she began to care for her in-laws. Because of this, she was asked to help with multiple friends and, later, Aunt Maggielene. During this time, she grew to feel the need to help others understand the responsibility, time, and the love and compassion required to take on the life of a caregiver.

Martha grew up in a small Southern Baptist Church. As a young family, she and Tony searched for a church home, eventually settling into Faith Bible Church, in Sharpsburg, Georgia, for the last twenty-two years. She worked sixteen years as a leader in their church's AWANA program along with being active in other church programs over the years.

With the support of her family, along with the encouragement of her caregiving and social worker friends, she remains confident in her family's decision to give her the opportunity to care for extended family and friends.

Printed in the USA
CPSIA information can be obtained
at www.ICGtesting.com
CBHW021352040824
12556CB00084B/509